Praise for Sue Palmer's
Toxic Childhood

'Practical, sensible and eminently attainable advice on how to detoxify childhood'

Deborah Orr, Independent

'A super child-rearing manual, founded in science, bolstered by much reading, a lot of interviews and a long career in education'

Times Educational Supplement

'Sue Palmer's *Toxic Childhood* is extensively researched, fluently written and easily read. It is a guidebook for parents, grandparents and all who care about present and future generations, as well as being an academic work in its own right'

Tribune

'A splendid book that draws together a vast swathe of the most authoritative research from a whole range of fields and disciplines ... that together explain "the worsening behaviour of children and the explosion in numbers of special needs pupils"'

The Mother magazine

'I could not put it down. It seemed to pull together all my worries about young children growing up in a fast-changing world, and yet ... the book is in fact very positive. The research it has drawn upon makes it a very powerful read. And, of course, it is written by a good writer in a very accessible way'

Early Childhood Practice

'A fascinating account of the problems facing kids today ... contains solid parenting advice on subjects ranging from diet to childcare'

Sainsbury's Magazine

'All too often we are told what is wrong with society/parenting/environment and more, but seldom told how we can so something to redress the balance ... This is what the author set out to do, and she has succeeded.

www.familyonwards.com

'A terrific book ... and so timely'

Anne Fine, author and former Children's Laureate

'Just what we all need to be reading. The levels of anxiety about our children are reaching new highs and we desperately need this kind of careful ...'

Dr R ... ry

'This is a compelling book, well researched and authoritative, with powerful messages in each of the chapters, and practical suggestions that are both helpful and realistic'

Marion Dowling, President of
the British Association of Early Childhood Education

'Essential reading for all those who work with children. It has fascinating and sometimes startling revelations about the damaging influences on the young within our society and offers some practical and very readable ideas and recommendations for all those who endeavour to give children the very best we can'

Gervase Phinn, author

'Almost every page in this book raises something compelling about the way we are treating children. It is a worrying book, but not unhopeful or unhelpful, and everyone concerned with children can rest assured that Sue Palmer is on their side'

Carousel

'Both refreshing and honest ... objectively considers an array of disciplines surrounding childhood and their underlying side effects. Then it integrates them and develops a clear and common goal for parents and others alike to jointly tackle the toxic environment that children are being exposed to ... Blame is not an issue of this book; it is about change and investing in the pivotal emotional needs of the young'

What About The Children?

'Every parent should read this book, as it does contain a wealth of information you should know'

Evening Herald

'One of the most talked about books on the market... teems with perceptive observations and sound advice'

Family Bulletin

'A brilliant book, Toxic Childhood, demonstrating how deprived children bear the brunt of rapid social change, and the knock-on effect this has on Britain's streets, schools and crime rate'

The Week

Detoxing Childhood

What Parents Need to Know to Raise
Happy, Successful Children

SUE PALMER

Copyright © Sue Palmer Ltd 2007

The right of Sue Palmer to be identified as
the author of this work has been asserted by her in accordance with the
Copyright, Designs and Patents Act 1988.

First published in trade paperback in Great Britain in 2007 by
Orion Books
an imprint of the Orion Publishing Group Ltd
Orion House, 5 Upper St Martin's Lane,
London WC2H 9EA
An Hachette Livre UK Company

3 5 7 9 10 8 6 4 2

A CIP catalogue record for this book is available
from the British Library.

ISBN: 978 0 7528 9010 4

Designed in Quadraat by Geoff Green Book Design

Printed in Great Britain by Clays

The Orion Publishing Group's policy is to use papers that are natural, renewable and recyclable
and made from wood grown in sustainable forests. The logging and manufacturing processes
are expected to conform to the environmental regulations of the country of origin.

Every effort has been made to fulfil requirements with regard to reproducing copyright material.
The author and publisher will be glad to rectify any omissions at the earliest opportunity.

Cartoons reproduced by kind permission of:

Pages 1 and 105: *The Spectator*. Page 2: © MATT/Telegraph Media Group. Page 4: © The New
Yorker Collection 1999 David Sipress from cartoonbank.com. All Rights Reserved.
Page 6: © Mark Anderson, www.andertoons.com. Page 8: Dave Coverly and Creators Syndicate,
Inc. Page 11: © The New Yorker Collection 2002 Matthew Diffee from cartoonbank.com.
All Rights Reserved. Page 61: © Morton Morland. Page 129: *Daily Mail* Mac Cartoon.
Page 141: Flying McCoys © 2005 Glenn and Gary McCoy. Distributed by Universal Press
Syndicate. Reprinted with permission. All rights reserved. Page 144: www.CartoonStock.com

www.orionbooks.co.uk

Contents

Author's Preface

During research for my book *Toxic Childhood* and in the months after its publication I met a great many experts on aspects of children's development. Like me, they were worried about the way side effects of modern life were affecting children. In September 2006 Dr Richard House, a specialist in child mental health, and I collected the signatures from 110 of them for the following letter to a national newspaper:

As professionals and academics from a range of backgrounds, we are deeply concerned at the escalating incidence of childhood depression and children's behavioural and developmental conditions. We believe this is largely due to a lack of understanding, on the part of both politicians and the general public, of the realities and subtleties of child development.

Since children's brains are still developing, they cannot adjust – as full-grown adults can – to the effects of ever more rapid technological and cultural change. They still need what developing human beings have always needed, including real food (as opposed to processed 'junk'), real play (as opposed to sedentary, screen-based entertainment), first-hand experience of the world they live in and regular interaction with the real-life significant adults in their lives.

They also need time. In a fast-moving hyper-competitive

culture, today's children are expected to cope with an ever-earlier start to formal schoolwork and an overly academic test-driven primary curriculum. They are pushed by market forces to act and dress like mini-adults and exposed via the electronic media to material which would have been considered unsuitable for children even in the very recent past.

Our society rightly takes great pains to protect children from physical harm, but seems to have lost sight of their emotional and social needs. However, it's now clear that the mental health of an unacceptable number of children is being unnecessarily compromised, and that this is almost certainly a key factor in the rise of substance abuse, violence and self-harm amongst our young people.

This is a complex socio-cultural problem to which there is no simple solution, but a sensible first step is to encourage parents and policy-makers to start talking about ways in which we can improve children's well-being. We therefore propose as a matter of urgency that

- public debate be initiated on child-rearing in the 21st century
- this issue should be central to public policy-making in coming decades.

The letter brought a flood of support and sparked a debate on childhood – not just in the UK but worldwide. It seemed that 'experts' weren't the only people feeling worried about the effects of a 21st-century lifestyle on children's development. But the plight of children in the UK is particularly alarming – in spring 2007, a report by UNICEF on a wide range of measures of childhood well-being found that British children are the unhappiest in the developed world.

All this made me want to write a short, easily accessible sequel to *Toxic Childhood*, showing parents how the negative influences on children's development can be defused. As a parent, I know that child-rearing doesn't leave much time for reading. And as an essentially optimistic soul, I'm much happier highlighting positive ways to detoxify childhood than stressing the negative effects of toxicity.

So *Detoxing Childhood* summarises the evidence and expands the advice for countering toxic childhood syndrome, gathered from experts around the globe. It is not an academic book, so I have not included references to the vast amount of research underpinning these recommendations – readers in search of an evidence base should consult *Toxic Childhood*. But it is – I hope – a much quicker, easier, more practical read than my original book.

In pulling these 'detox' suggestions together, I'm deeply indebted to:

- the many academics who advised me, during the *Toxic Childhood* research and since publication
- the thousands of parents and teachers I've met over the last year, who have provided practical insights and ideas for detoxification.

It would be hopeless trying to list them all and, anyway, in most cases I fear I have no idea of their names, so this book contains no specific acknowledgements. It is, however, dedicated to those academics, teachers and – above all – parents, with huge admiration for their work in the vital task of detoxing 21st-century childhood.

Sue Palmer
www.suepalmer.co.uk

Introduction

In the last 20 or so years, the lifestyles of UK families have changed beyond recognition.

Back in the mid-1980s, all-day TV was a novelty, few families owned a computer, and the phone was tethered by a wire to the wall. Mum was usually at home (and in the kitchen), while children played games outside.

Two decades later, most families have 24-hour multi-channel TV coverage, access to the whole world via the internet, and mobile phones that also take photographs and record videos. The majority of mothers are out at work – with knock-on effects on the family diet and routine – while children are more likely to be indoors, watching TV or chatting on MSN. Play now happens indoors on a PlayStation, games on a Gameboy.

The speed of technological and cultural changes has been so fast that we haven't really had time to think about it. And since, for most adults, the changes have been generally welcome, we haven't really bothered to think. But it's now becoming clear that some aspects of modern life are seriously damaging our children.

The trouble is that our lifestyles may have

changed, but the basic blueprint for the human brain hasn't – evolution is a very slow process. So today's children are still the same small, vulnerable creatures that they've always been and, in order to grow up bright, balanced and healthy, they still have the same basic needs.

What do children need?

The way human beings develop depends largely on our genes; our bodies and brains are 'hard wired' for certain types of behaviour. For instance, unless there's something seriously wrong, all children learn to walk and talk.

But the way we bring up children also affects development. Even those with perfectly wired brains need to practise walking and talking – if they don't have enough opportunities to move or communicate, they won't make as much progress as they should.

So what do children need to grow into bright, balanced adults? Over the last few decades scientists have learned a great deal about the workings of the brain, identifying four major strands to human development through childhood. These four strands (opposite) aren't independent of each other – they overlap and interweave. If a child's daily routine supports their development, that child should grow steadily healthier, more balanced and better equipped in every way to make his or her way in the world.

But if a child's lifestyle doesn't support this overall development they may well have problems as they grow older.

'How did sports day go?'

Physical development

For body and brain to grow strong and healthy, children need a warm, safe home, good wholesome food, fresh air and exercise, and plenty of sleep. These are the basics upon which all other development depends.

Emotional development

To develop the emotional resilience needed to thrive in a complex modern world, children need to feel loved, valued and secure. This starts with a strong attachment bond between mother and child (see pages 68–9). As children grow, they need a balance of warmth (loving attention) and firmness (clear boundaries for behaviour) to keep them safe. The inner sense of security this inspires helps develop a resilient child with high self-esteem and staying power.

Social development

Social development is also rooted in a secure, happy family life. Then, as children grow older, they need to mix with a wider range of people – and especially to play, without too much adult interference, with other children. This is how they learn to get along with other people. They also need to learn how to behave in institutional life, starting with school, and to balance their own needs with the needs of society as a whole.

Cognitive development

Cognitive development (the capacity to think and learn) is dependent on physical, emotional and social experiences. From their earliest days, children need

- first-hand experiences of their world – seeing, hearing, touching, smelling, tasting, exploring – to spark their curiosity and support understanding
- plenty of interaction with the important adults in their lives, including songs, rhymes and stories to develop language skills
- opportunities for creative, imaginative play, including play with other children.

Gradually, as firm physical, emotional, social and linguistic foundations are laid, they become ready for more formal learning at school. This includes the three Rs of reading, writing and reckoning, important for further cognitive development.

The loss of child-rearing wisdom

Part of the problem with modern child-rearing is that as women's roles in society have changed essential knowledge has been forgotten.

In the past, bringing up children was always 'women's work', and through the centuries women learned a lot about their charges. Information about children's needs was passed from mother to daughter, backed up by grandmothers and other 'wise women' in the local community.

In the revolutionary change of the last few decades, much of this ancient wisdom has disappeared. As families and tight-knit communities splintered apart, the chain of information was broken. And as women gained in education and independence, they left the home for the workplace. By the end of the 20th century, no one valued traditional 'women's work' – and anyway, the world was changing so rapidly that ancient wisdom didn't seem to apply any more.

Gradually, however, science has confirmed that much of the ancient wisdom was true. In a fast-moving, technology-driven society, many children's developmental needs are not being met. Instead, unintended side-effects of modern life swirl together to create 'toxic childhood syndrome' (opposite).

"Your mother and I are feeling overwhelmed, so you'll have to bring yourselves up."

Physical toxicity

A great many – probably a majority – of our children have developed a taste for unhealthy food and a couch-potato screen-based lifestyle, and have related problems with sleeping.

Emotional toxicity

When parents are busy juggling work and domestic responsibilities, children often miss out on the family time that breeds emotional security, including early attachment (see page 69) and regular routines for mealtimes, bedtimes and so on. In a confused and confusing world, many parents now find it difficult to set and maintain firm boundaries for their children's behaviour. Exposure to screen-based violence can be emotionally destabilising, and family breakdown – massively on the increase – can cause serious and long-lasting distress.

Social toxicity

Lack of family time and involvement can mean children aren't as well prepared for social life outside home. And since they seldom play unsupervised they don't learn naturally how to make friends, take turns and deal with problems. Growing up in an electronic village rather than a real one means they're influenced as never before by marketeers, unsuitable role models and celebrity culture.

Cognitive toxicity

Instead of first-hand, real-life experiences, many children's lives are now built around screen-based entertainment. Less time spent with real-life adults and playmates means poorer language development and, in a consumer culture, creative play has often given way to 'toy consumption'.

Conditions may be no less toxic once children start school. In today's competitive world many schools have been turned into 'standards factories', driven by government tests and targets; teachers don't have the time to provide opportunities for play and talk. And health and safety regulations coupled with fear of litigation have curtailed first-hand experiences such as outdoor education and field trips.

Too much too soon?

The loss of wisdom about childcare has led to another problem. In a quick-fire quick-fix culture, it's easy to imagine that children can grow up faster, too. But children develop over time; you can't speed up the growth of an organism as complex as a human being.

In terms of physical growth, this is obvious. Babies start off tiny and grow bigger with the passing years – no one would suggest stretching children on a rack to make them grow more quickly. But psychological growth happens out of sight. Children's emotional, social and cognitive development isn't so obvious. The only gauge of their maturity is their outward behaviour, and this is often misleading.

For instance, all children want to seem grown-up, so they copy adult actions and language even though they don't really understand it. Today's children see and hear plenty of adult models on TV, and they're quick to pick up streetwise behaviour and catchphrases that make them appear old beyond their years. They are also deeply influenced by the contemporary culture of 'cool'. This decrees that, at all times, you must seem unconcerned and worldly wise: however unsettling you find something, you mustn't let on. So even though many children are emotionally unsettled by the stuff they see on TV (especially frightening items on the news) or domestic dramas at home, they appear to be fine, accepting everything we throw at them with a sophisticated shrug.

"How expensive would it be to just
skip practice and get right to perfect?"

Most parents quite like the thought that their children's minds are maturing faster. 'Kids today grow up so quickly,' we say, proud of our offspring's apparent sophistication. But genuine emotional resilience and social competence are not so quickly won. They develop gradually through confidence in dealing with the real world and satisfying real-life relationships with family and friends. Today's children may look and act big, but often they are extremely fragile inside.

Our tests-and-targets educational system adds to this 'too much too soon' mentality. In an increasingly competitive world, government ministers urge schools to start children on formal learning earlier and earlier. To politicians it seems a good idea to push children to achieve more when they're young, so they get 'a head start' on children in other countries. In fact, concentrating on children's cognitive development at the expense of other aspects of psychological growth can be deeply damaging in the long run.

In fact, attempts to speed up cognitive and emotional development almost always end in tears, perhaps many years down the line. Antisocial behaviour and mental health problems in the teenage years (such as binge-drinking, drug abuse, depression and anorexia) usually have their roots in childhood stress. It is no coincidence that Britain now has worse problems among teenagers than any other country in Europe.

Childhood is not a race

This is not to say that we should hold children back. Holding them back would be just as harmful as expecting them to run before they can walk, or to write before they can talk. We need to encourage interests and nurture progress. But we also have to recognise that children are different and develop at different rates.

Some differences are down to our genes. For instance, boys and girls develop in different ways at different speeds. The male of the species was originally destined to spend time out hunting on the open plains rather than communic-ating back at camp, so boys tend to be slower at language and more interested in outdoor physical play. With time, loving attention and the right sorts of experiences, they'll eventually be just as good as girls at communication and small-scale 'indoor' skills. Similarly girls, when given support, praise and opportunities to practise, can equal boys in risk-taking and large-scale physical coordination.

But in a competitive consumer culture, 21st-century parents tend to want our children to be the quickest, the cleverest, the winners. So instead of giving them the chance to develop into well-rounded, balanced human beings, we turn childhood into a competitive struggle.

Of course, competition can sometimes be healthy; it's a key force behind human progress. But collaboration is important, too, and in the past mothers used to discuss their problems and swap advice around the tea table or in the washhouse. As competitive consumerism grew during the 20th century, such collaboration waned, and as women honed their competitive skills in the aggressive masculine world of the workplace, it all but disappeared.

Children have often become an extension of their parents' ambition, to be cheered on in a competitive race. But this is a race in which both winners and losers can suffer. Children pushed to achieve for their parents' benefit may win in the short term, but if they're pushed too hard the emotional stress can lead to long-term harm. As for the losers – well, all too often they just give up the unequal struggle and find some other way to assert their individuality.

In a wider social context, competitive parenting creates an ever greater divide between haves and have-nots. Middle-class parents frantically trying to ensure their own offspring emerge as winners have little time to worry about the effects of the system on children from disadvantaged backgrounds. They start worrying ten or fifteen years later, when these 'born losers' have turned into hoodies hanging menacingly round the shopping centre, drug addicts relying on crime to feed their habit, or teenage mothers clogging up the benefits system.

> Our fundamental problem today is a lack of common feeling between people – the notion that life is essentially a competitive struggle. With such a philosophy, the losers become alienated, and even the winners can't relax in peace.
>
> Lord Richard Layard, professor of economics

And it's not just competitive politicians or parents that cause this damage – it's our competitive culture. Growing up in an electronic village, children themselves are soon caught up in the race, convinced by marketeers that success is measured in consumer 'must-haves'. Many children now believe that what you are is what you own, a philosophy that breeds happiness for neither winner nor loser.

Can we detoxify childhood?

Fortunately, the human brain is a remarkable organ, and even when something goes awry it can usually be reprogrammed to overcome the problem. We *can* detoxify childhood. But first we have to acknowledge that something is wrong. At present, some parents refuse to accept that contemporary childhood is anything other than perfect.

Their reluctance may be due to fear of seeming old-codgerish (people have been saying that 'the younger generation is going to the dogs' since Cain killed Abel) and suggesting that the modern world is somehow 'bad'. But you don't have to be a grumpy old person or a raving technophobe to recognise that even the greatest leaps forward in human progress can bring with them unintended side effects.

Some people – especially women – may fear that addressing the problem means going back to the childcare arrangements of the past, when mothers were trapped by marriage and custom into a lifetime of domestic drudgery. But if we're seriously to detox childhood for the 21st century, we have to find ways *forward* that enhance the lives of men, women and children.

It's also easy to fall into paralysing fatalism. The problems seem so wide-ranging, so ingrained in our culture – how can we change the behaviour of marketeers, media magnates, big business? But ours is a very enterprising species – we've overcome far worse problems in the past. In fact, it's less than two centuries since Britain underwent several decades of massive social and technological change called the Industrial Revolution. While this brought great advances, it also caused terrible suffering, especially for children. But as people woke up to the problems, they found ways round them, leading to massive improvements in all children's lives. There's no reason why we can't do this again, and with the benefit of new technology, we should be able to put things right much more quickly.

Parental love is the greatest force on the planet. When parents know what's good for their children, and what does them harm, they *will* act. With any luck they'll act collaboratively, and influence others in society to act, too. By detoxing childhood, we could detox the whole global electronic village.

So why not start today?

Section 1

Detoxing Parenthood

*"Before we begin this family meeting, how about we go around
and say our names and a little something about ourselves."*

Twenty-first Century Parents

Being a parent has always been hard work. Looking after children is physically and emotionally draining, it goes on 24 hours a day, 365 days a year, and the stakes – in terms of your offspring's future happiness – are high.

But being a parent in a fast-moving electronic global village is harder than ever. Most parents today are trying to juggle the job with similarly exhausting paid employment. They're also fighting a constant battle against marketing and peer-group pressures, they're bombarded with worrying news and statistics about children and – as toxic childhood syndrome spreads – they're blamed by government and the media.

So it's not surprising if parents feel battered and browbeaten. Or that, since many of the causes of toxic childhood syndrome seem beyond their control, they're also bewildered about how to get out of the mess. But for the sake of their children, and the world those children will grow up and live in, parents have to get their act together. Detoxing parenthood is the first step to detoxing childhood.

Parents in charge

This chapter looks at how 21st-century lifestyles make it more difficult for parents to meet children's needs in terms of diet, sleep, day-to-day family life, exercise and play. It gives some suggestions for detoxing children's lives, expanded from the expert advice in *Toxic Childhood*.

They are only suggestions. All children are different – some need more warmth or a firmer hand than others. This is why following the advice of parenting experts, especially those who lay down very hard and fast rules, can sometimes be counterproductive. Parents *have* to make their own decisions about the best ways to handle their own children. To make good decisions they need to know

- what children need for healthy development
- how modern life can prevent these needs being met.

The parental balancing act

There's now a huge body of research showing that to raise happy, resilient children in a modern democratic society, parents need to balance warmth with firmness.

Warmth	Firmness
Giving children time, love and attention	Setting clear boundaries for behaviour
Listening to them and taking their feelings and opinions into account	Translating these boundaries into rules and routines for the family
Helping children feel good about themselves	Insisting that children follow the rules

If you can achieve this balance, you're an **authoritative** parent, and your children are likely to feel good about themselves, to get along with other people and to behave well at school. As they grow older, they develop self-discipline, which means they enter their teens able to make their own decisions and resist temptation.

So it pays to be authoritative. But it's not easy to achieve the balance, as you have to make constant adjustments depending on the circumstances.

What if you get the balance wrong?

Parents who are firm but not warm are **authoritarian**. Their children may be well behaved at home, but lacking in self-esteem. Since they never learn to think for themselves, they're likely to go off the rails when the parent isn't there, particularly in the teenage years.

Parents who are warm but not firm are **indulgent**. Their children usually have high self-esteem – sometimes too high. They may have problems making and keeping friends, or following rules, since they see themselves as more important than other people. They are also likely to lack self-discipline, and thus are prey to temptation and peer pressure during the teenage years.

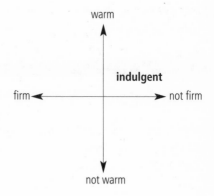

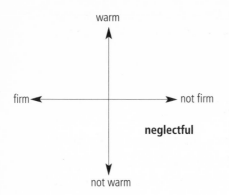

Parents who are neither warm nor firm are **neglectful**. Their children are seriously at risk. They tend to have low self-esteem, poor self-discipline and little respect for the feelings of others. They are highly likely to be disturbed teenagers and unhappy adults.

What about the children?

To achieve an authoritative parenting style, it helps to know something about the way children's brains develop and how they learn. As the eminent neuroscientist Susan Greenfield has pointed out, the human brain has not changed since Cro-Magnon times. Every baby is born a little Stone Age baby, and learns in the same way. Over childhood, we help build the brain structures that will help our off-spring survive in a complex 21st-century culture...

Only connect

When a baby is born, it has almost its full consignment of brain cells – around a billion. But what matter are the connections between the cells, and the vast majority of these are formed after birth, in response to the baby's experiences.

The scientific name for brain cells is 'neurons', and the connections forged between the cells are known as 'neural pathways' joining up into 'neural networks'. These underpin all human behaviour; for instance, almost all human children develop the neural networks required to smile, laugh, feed themselves, walk and talk.

Children build up their basic neural networks gradually, through constant repetition of particular experiences, until a pattern is firmly established and the activity becomes as natural to them as breathing.

By this time, the network is so deeply embedded it has become part of their brain structure. In the words of one neuroscientist, 'cells that fire together wire together'.

Use it or lose it

But the brain has to be selective. If neurons don't fire and wire, they'll eventually disappear. For instance, a baby is born with all the neurons it needs to speak any language on earth, but the sounds that baby will learn are those of the language it hears every day (not surprisingly known as its 'mother tongue'). The neurons for picking up other language sounds die away, so that after the age of about six the brain can no longer discriminate them. This is why, when they learn English as adults, Chinese people find it so difficult to pronounce the sound 'r'. It doesn't exist in their language, so the neurons required to hear and pronounce it have disappeared.

Building better brains

The experiences of childhood create the adult brain. Between birth and three, children slowly lay the foundations – learning to move, communicate, balance and control their bodies and actions. This is an enormous amount of learning, more than they'll learn at any other time in their lives. Indeed, it underpins everything they will become in the future. If they can establish strong healthy neural networks – learning through pleasurable interaction with loving adults – all their later learning will be built on solid foundations.

Once the foundations are laid, we tend to forget about them; foundations are by their very nature buried underground, so most people are utterly unaware of their importance. Most of us don't remember much about the next stage of learning either – between three and six. Neural networks continue to be formed at an amazing rate during these years, too.

Learning for three- to six-year-olds is still very much embedded in first-hand experience, but as their language develops they're more able to learn through discussing what they see and do. And they're more able to learn in a group, getting along with other children at pre-school. Their experiences at this stage underpin their schooling, and can make the difference between long-term success and failure in education.

After the age of about six, children are ready for more formal learning at school. Neural networks continue to develop, but it's more difficult to start them from scratch – the stronger the foundations, the more easily the child will learn.

Success, motivation and rewards

All this means we need to give children lots of opportunities to learn at the right level for them. If an activity is at the right level, children succeed. Then they want to repeat it, and repetition of healthy activity builds a healthy brain.

Every successful action embeds the neural network a little more deeply. On the other hand, failure weakens the network, meaning the child is less likely to want to repeat that experience. If we ask children to do something that's beyond their capabilities, we can demotivate them.

Motivation drives learning, and the greatest motivation for a young child is parental attention. If we reward children with cuddles, smiles, interest and praise, they learn quickly. At the same time, the parent shares the pleasure of their child's success, so it's a win-win situation. But if children aren't rewarded in this way, they'll usually seek some other means of satisfaction, and all too often they discover that mis-behaviour attracts plenty of attention. Then parents have the problem of training their offspring out of bad behaviour and into good behaviour. On the whole, it's quicker to start as you mean to go on.

Oo, oo, oo, I want to be like you-oo

Imitation is one of the earliest human instincts. If you put your tongue out at a newborn baby, the baby will obligingly stick out its tongue at you. As children develop increasing control over their bodies, they imitate us more and more. It's no coincidence that they eventually end up walking and talking. (The odd 'feral child' has been discovered, reared by dogs or wolves. They move about on all fours and growl.)

As they grow older, children continue to copy what they see and hear, so if you want them to take off their boots at the back door, take off yours; if you want them to address you politely, make sure you model politeness in the way you speak to them. But remember that it's not just you they'll copy. If they watch a lot of violent, aggressive TV shows, or shows where children are cheeky to adults, they'll pick up behaviour and language from them.

Repetition, repetition, repetition

To sum up, what happens during childhood, and particularly early childhood, forms the basis of all our habits – habits of mind, habits of behaviour, eating habits, sleeping habits, learning habits. So the experiences we give our children influence their behaviour and personality for the rest of their lives.

This is why routine is so important in a family home; pleasant, comfortable routines develop feelings of security, making for a happy child. Once established, they also ensure that family life runs smoothly for everyone. And once something's become a habit, you don't have to think about it, so every good habit is one less thing to think about in a busy day.

On the other hand, bad habits can be difficult to break. If children start eating junk food, getting to bed late, watching too much TV and copying the behaviour of people they see on it, parents (and later teachers) will struggle to control their behaviour.

So the suggestions here are aimed at avoiding bad habits and forming good ones. But they are just suggestions. The experts who gave them don't know you or your child, and neither do I. In the end, parents (and other adults in charge of children) must make their own decisions, day by day, year by year.

The more you know about child development, and the more you are aware of the possibilities and dangers of modern life, the more confident you'll be to do it your way.

1. Eating Habits

Thanks to campaigners like Jamie Oliver, we already know that a 21st-century junk food diet can damage children's physical development. But there's less public awareness of the damage junk food can do to the developing brain.

How can diet damage the brain?

Too much sugar Sugary drinks and snacks provide an instant 'sugar high' which can make some children hyperactive. When the high wears off, they feel low and cranky, so they crave more sugar to lift them again. But sugary foods don't provide the vitamins, minerals and nutrients children need for normal brain functions.	**A cocktail of additives** When children eat a wide variety of processed foods they take in a cocktail of additives. Little is known about how additives act in combination – but experts suspect different combinations can have adverse effects on brain chemistry, and these effects may vary from child to child. The best advice is simply to avoid too many processed foods and drinks.
Omega 3 deficit Human brains and bodies need Omega 3 fatty acids (found mainly in oily fish) to work properly – in terms of brain function, they seem to help 'oil the wheels' of neural activity. The human body can't make fatty acids itself, so we have to find them in our food. But as fish has become a less significant part of the Western diet, many children aren't getting enough Omega 3.	**The wrong sort of fats** Many processed foods contain transfats (often listed on the label as 'hydrogenated vegetable oil'). There's growing evidence that transfats pose many health risks to adults and children. Some researchers suspect that the transfatty acids they contain actually clog up the brain rather than lubricating it.

'If we do not pay attention to the diets of our children, we may be faced with a future of brain degenerating problems which are closely linked to learning problems.'

International symposium on brain research and learning, 2003

Growing up in a junk food jungle

In a multimedia consumer-driven world, it's not just parents who feed their children, it's the whole culture. Parents may know what their offspring *ought* to be eating, but it's not what 21st-century culture has programmed children to want.

Over the last 20 years, diets have become more processed, junk food more prevalent. Marketing messages pushing unhealthy food are everywhere children look – on TV, on the internet, on billboards and vending machines. Even schools have been lured into promoting unhealthy snacks to help pay their bills.

Once children have developed a taste for unhealthy stuff, it can be almost an addiction – other foods begin to taste bland and unappetising. Weaning children off junk food can be a difficult business.

If you're a new parent, start as you mean to go on. For instance:

- Give babies and toddlers only water or milk to drink so they don't develop a taste for sugary drinks
- Introduce your child to a variety of real (mashed up) food, rather than processed ready-meals.

How can parents take control?

The general advice of the experts on diet and nutrition that I consulted was this:

- Ensure children eat regular meals, rather than graze on snack foods
- Serve meals cooked from fresh ingredients rather than processed food
- Follow dietary guidelines, such as the food pyramid overleaf
- Don't have any junk food, snacks or sugary drinks in the house (see page 27)
- Explain to children why you want them to eat healthy food and why they should be wary of advertising messages ('We love you; the marketeers just want your money!')
- Don't make junk food into 'forbidden fruit' by banning it altogether – allow occasional burgers and so on when away from home
- BUT don't make it into a 'special treat' – treat it with the disdain it deserves
- Set a good example – detoxing your child's diet is a good opportunity to sort out your own eating habits

Use the food pyramid to ensure your child gets a healthy balanced daily diet.

- The foods in the bottom layer (bread, rice, etc) should provide about 40% of the diet.
- Those in the second layer (fruit and vegetables) should provide 30%.
- Foods in the third layer (dairy, meat, fish, etc) should provide around 20%.
- The items at the tip of the pyramid should be taken sparingly – and should make up no more than 10% of the daily diet (but young children **do** need full fat milk, so don't put preschoolers on skimmed milk).

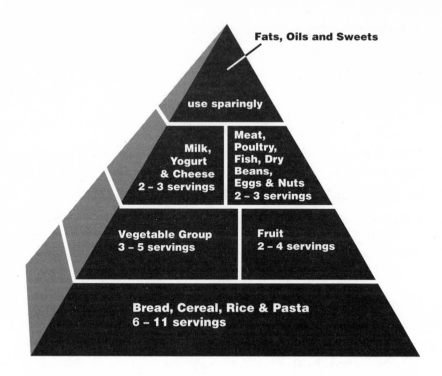

Fats, Oils and Sweets

use sparingly

Milk, Yogurt & Cheese
2 – 3 servings

Meat, Poultry, Fish, Dry Beans, Eggs & Nuts
2 – 3 servings

Vegetable Group
3 – 5 servings

Fruit
2 – 4 servings

Bread, Cereal, Rice & Pasta
6 – 11 servings

Eating together

A key factor in taking control of what children eat is to provide regular family meals, where you – not some marketing executive – are in charge of their diet.

For working parents this is obviously difficult and it may be that, on some days at least, a parent-substitute has to supervise mealtimes. But whatever your childcare arrangements (see Section II) the key is eating together.

Why shared meals are important

- Parents are in charge of the menu and so can ensure healthy food and train their children to eat it.

- Regular meals, served at the same time each day, help give children the security essential for healthy development.
- It's an opportunity for talk, improving children's social and communication skills.
- It's a time for forging strong family bonds.

> 'They're not called eating habits for nothing. Habits are ways of behaving that have become very deep-seated and are therefore difficult to change. Habits acquired in childhood tend to stay with you life long.'
>
> Dr Susan Jebb, nutritionist

Social eating

The people you eat with needn't be confined to the immediate family. In fact, people I meet from Mediterranean or Asian backgrounds usually rhapsodise about the pleasure of sharing with extended family and friends. They tend to value the social aspect of eating, just as they value fresh, well-cooked food, far more than British or American families.

While extended families are thin on the ground these days in the UK, most parents have a network of friends who may enjoy sharing meals with them. Three mothers I met in Lancashire had started a 'children's supper club' on a Wednesday evening. Two of them were single mums and one had a husband who was back from work too late to eat with the children during the week. They all felt they needed adult company, so they started a rota, and now take turns to feed all three broods once a week. It's easy enough to produce nursery food such as shepherd's pie or pasta in industrial quantities, it means two out of three mums get a break from cooking on Wednesday, and everyone enjoys the conviviality. In fact, they were thinking of extending it to two or three evenings a week.

How to wean children off unhealthy food

- Offer a mixture of new foods and the healthiest of children's old favourites.
- Let your child help prepare homemade burgers, pasta sauce, fishcakes, etc., instead of having processed ones.
- Make the food look attractive to children, e.g. use pastry cutters to make interesting shapes, make faces on the plate, experiment with E-number-free food colouring.
- Use marketing tricks, such as giving dishes interesting-sounding names (Cheesy Special, Sardine Heaven).
- Chop or mince less-liked vegetables in the food processor to disguise their presence in soups, stews, casseroles and so on.
- Make healthy finger food, such as raw vegetables with a dip.
- Serve fresh fruit for dessert – bake it, stew it, peel and cut it into shapes. Let your child make a fruit salad.
- Involve your child in planning and preparing food as much as you can. If they can be involved in growing it, that's even better!

To cook for family and friends is an act of love that binds together all who share it. A family that eats together is more likely to be a kind close family where children will grow up to be kind and considerate.

Raymond Blanc, chef

Don't panic if your child goes through a 'fussy stage' – eating an unbalanced diet for a while isn't likely to do any damage. But battles over food do. Apart from making mealtimes unpleasant, they can set up problems with eating in later years.

Cutting back on snack attack

Most junk food comes in the form of tasty snacks, needing little or no preparation and easy to eat with the fingers. The high levels of salt and sugar make them addictive, so children tend to enjoy grazing on such snacks throughout the day.

But children kept topped up with snacks or sugary drinks will be less interested in anything on offer at the table, and more difficult to wean off unhealthy food. Changing your family's eating habits means cutting back on 'snack attack':

- Don't have any junk snacks or sugary drinks in the house – if they're not available, no one can be tempted.
- Have a rule that no one snacks for, say, two hours before meals.
- For other occasions, keep a list of healthy snacks and the ingredients to provide them, e.g.

  fresh and dried fruit

  yogurt

  buttered toast

  plain popcorn

  boiled egg and soldiers

  crackers with cheese or peanut butter

  raisin bread or fruit loaf

  toasted muffins

  dips and biscuits or vegetable sticks

  plain biscuits, scones or buns

'Adults decide WHAT, WHEN and WHERE children should eat. Children decide HOW MUCH, and even WHETHER.'

Ellyn Satter, nutritionist

Detoxing mealtimes

Be warm:

- Make family meals pleasurable social occasions.

- Involve your child in planning, shopping for and preparing meals whenever possible.

- Serve food in serving dishes (rather than putting it on your child's plate) so s/he can choose portion size.

- Don't insist on your child eating anything. Provide plenty of bread / vegetables / pasta / rice so s/he doesn't go hungry.

- When you introduce a new food, just offer 'a little taste' and if your child doesn't like it, don't push it. (If s/he does, give lots of praise.)

- When you next serve that dish, offer another 'little taste', explaining that one's tastes change as one grows up.

- *Expect* your child to eat and behave well at mealtimes and give plenty of praise as s/he masters manners, stressing how grown up this is.

- Involve your child in mealtime conversation (see next page and page 88).

Be firm:

- Eat meals at a regular time each day, at a table in a TV-free zone.

- Don't allow anyone to snack for at least two hours before the meal, so the family comes to the table hungry (snacking before meals is rude to the cook).

- No snacking after meals either. If your child doesn't want to eat, s/he'll have to live with hunger.

- You choose which dishes to serve, because you know what's nutritious and good for your child.

- Don't make special dishes – everyone eats the same food.

- No sugary drinks, just water (adults may have beer or wine if they wish, because they're adults).

- Introduce table manners gradually, focusing on one aspect at a time.

- Don't give rewards for eating particular foods or for good behaviour.

- Once your child is trained up, insist on good table manners, e.g. not starting till everyone (including the cook) is sitting down, 'pleases' and 'thank yous', passing to others before serving oneself.

Table talk

Mealtimes are a great opportunity for family talk (see page 90) and if conversation flags, you can always play word or memory games. One family told me they sometimes try to talk for five minutes without anyone saying the word 'no'. 'Surprisingly fun,' they said, 'and educational for adults and children alike.'

But while it's important to involve children in conversation, they must also know not to interrupt adults' conversations. 'The more the merrier' is especially true around a dining table – sharing meals with other families means more adults and children for everyone to chat to, so no one feels left out.

Further reading

On childhood nutrition: Alex Richardson, *They Are What You Feed Them* (HarperCollins, 2006).

On breaking bad habits: Ellyn Satter, *Child of Mine: Feeding with Love and Good Sense* (Bull Publishing, 2000).

Netmums and Judith Wills, *Feeding Kids: 120 Foolproof Family Recipes (The Netmums Cookery Book)* (Headline, 2007).

Useful websites

Independent research findings on food and behaviour:
    www.FABresearch.org

Latest US food guidelines: www.mypyramid.gov

The US Center for Science in Public Interest: www.cspinet.org

Campaign to stop junk food advertising:
    www.childrensfoodcampaign.co.uk

2. Sleeping Habits

Another key ingredient in toxic childhood syndrome is lack of sleep. Children today sleep for around one and a half hours less per night than children twenty years ago.

As a society we no longer value sleep. Success is measured in terms of constant activity; the busier you are, the more successful you're perceived to be. So sleep seems a waste of valuable time, and being able to survive on very little is often portrayed in the media as a strength.

Why children need sleep

In fact, scientists have recently discovered that sleep plays a very significant part in learning and memory. Good sleeping habits are therefore important for all of us, particularly children:

- Information and skills learned during the day are transferred into long-term memory during sleep. Children learn a great deal every day, so they need plenty of sleep to consolidate it.
- Sleep is essential for physical growth too, and children are still growing.
- Lack of sleep makes children cranky and irritable, leading to poor attention and bad behaviour both at home and school.

Why are children sleeping less?

- Working parents, arriving home late, may delay bedtime so as to spend more time with their children.
- Children stay awake to watch TV, spend time on game consoles or in chat rooms, especially if this electronic equipment is in their bedrooms.
- 21st-century children find it more difficult to go to sleep, probably due to a combination of
  - ★ diet (additives such caffeine, found in most soft drinks, increase wakefulness)
  - ★ lack of physical exercise
  - ★ over-stimulation of the brain from fast-moving screen-based entertainment
  - ★ lack of routine, including a gradual wind-down to bedtime
  - ★ lack of parental attention as part of the bedtime routine, leading to attention-seeking behaviour
- Children who are emotionally disturbed often have trouble sleeping. Stress over schoolwork, worries over disturbing TV programmes (especially if watched in the bedroom before sleep) or anxiety about family problems can all keep children awake.
- Many children develop poor sleeping habits from the very start, because parents don't know how to establish good ones early on.

How much sleep do children need?

Age group	Recommended hours of sleep
Babies (3–11 months)	14–15 (over 24 hours)
Toddlers (12–35 months)	12–14
Pre-schoolers(3–6 years)	11–13
Primary school age (7–12 years)	10–11

Stopping bad habits before they begin

The sleeping habits children learn as babies can affect them for the rest of their lives. As with diet, the best advice is to start as you mean to go on. If you're a new parent:

- Ensure a calm and quiet end to the day – dim the light so your baby begins to associate this time with sleep.
- Help your baby become a 'self-soother' by putting him/her down to sleep when drowsy. Babies who learn to fall asleep by themselves are more likely to settle back down on their own if they wake up in the night.
- Once your baby has started to sleep through the night, if s/he wakes don't rush to pick him/her up immediately – give a couple of minutes for him/her to settle without your help.
- Develop day- and night-time sleep schedules and stick to them. The more stable your routine, the easier your baby will find it to settle down at bedtime.
- Don't underestimate the importance of daytime naps (babies need them to consolidate the huge amount of learning they do every day). Make sure your baby gets regular naps even though it might sometimes be inconvenient.

If parents don't establish good sleeping habits for their children, it can become a huge problem for the whole family. Sleepy children are cranky and unpleasant, so their behaviour deteriorates in the evening – and the more tired a child is, the more difficult it can be to settle them for sleep.

After a long day, parents need time to relax together, not a long evening attempting to get a recalcitrant child to sleep. It really is worth putting thought and effort into developing and retaining a restful bedtime routine (see page 35).

The monsters in the bedroom

One of the most disturbing developments of recent years has been the movement of electronic equipment – TVs, computers and so on – into children's bedrooms. These things have no place in the quiet, darkened room prescribed by all the sleep specialists. There are many other reasons that bedrooms should not become 'virtual worlds' (see page 108), but the effects on children's sleeping patterns should be enough to convince us to reverse this trend.

Bedrooms are for sleeping, and electronic equipment interferes with sleep:

- Human beings are programmed to sleep in the dark. Light and noise from TVs, computer screens, etc. can reset the body clock, changing the sleep/wake cycle and causing lifelong sleep problems.
- Electronic lights (and possibly emissions from mobile phones) block the body's secretion of the sleep hormone so children don't feel sleepy. Research suggests this may have many long-term health consequences.
- TV and computer use just before sleep leaves children in a state of heightened alertness so they find it more difficult to settle.
- Many children stay awake (often without parents' knowledge) watching TV, playing games and so on late into the night.
- Children often text each other on mobile phones or send chatroom messages late at night: your child might be sleeping less deeply because s/he's waiting for messages from friends.
- Many children now watch bedtime TV rather than sharing a bedtime story, songs and chat with parents. This is a serious erosion of important family time.

I'm always stunned when parents tell me 'Oh yes, as soon as we say "Lights out" his TV goes off and that's it till the next day!' Were they never children themselves? Did they never read under the covers with a torch? I can assure all parents that when you're not there, your little darling is doing all sorts of things he or she is not allowed to do. It's part of growing up. So when we *really* don't want them to do it, we have to make it impossible.

> Good sleep habits don't happen by accident. Parents have to show their children how to sleep.   Tessa Livingstone, executive producer of BBC's *Child of Our Time*

Helping good habits to stick

Make sure a bedtime routine (such as the one opposite) is well established before interrupting it with holidays, trips or late-night excursions. If not, you might have to start the whole training programme again from scratch. Even on holiday, try to keep to the routine as much as possible. Late nights are generally not good for children.

Many children go through phases when their sleep patterns are disturbed, but the key is to nip these in the bud so they don't turn into a bad habit. For instance, one mother whose son suddenly took to night-time waking and wandering told me how she used a star chart: one star for every night of staying abed, with a prize for seven consecutive stars. By the time her child had managed a full week in order to win his prize, the wandering habit was broken and the good habit of sleeping through the night re-established.

Detoxing bedtime

Be warm:

- Make sure your child's bedroom is comfortable, welcoming ... and *cool*, so the bed is cosy and inviting.
- Devise a bedtime ritual that you and your child enjoy, for instance:
  - ★ a drink of warm milk
  - ★ bathtime, teeth-cleaning, etc.
  - ★ lullabies or soft music (the same tunes every night can condition a child to feel sleepy)
  - ★ a short chat about the day
  - ★ a bedtime story
  - ★ a security object, such as a blanket or teddy
  - ★ your special way of saying goodnight, and your goodnight kiss.
- Listen and respond to your child's bedtime fears. For instance, if your child is scared of monsters, give the room a spray with Monster Repellent (a water-filled plant spray).
- If your child is scared of the dark, listen to him/her and talk about these fears and try to allay them. If s/he really can't manage without a nightlight, get the dimmest you can and put it well away from the bed.

Be firm:

- No televisions or other electronic equipment in the bedroom.
- No additive-rich foods at teatime (especially no fizzy drinks high in caffeine).
- Bedtime is bedtime – no staying up late (except on *very* special occasions). Adjust bedtimes as your child gets older, on the basis of scientific recommendations (see page 31).
- Begin the wind-down half an hour or so before bedtime by removing your child from TV or other technological distractions.
- Decide how long you'll stay with your child as part of the bedtime ritual and stick to it, perhaps setting a timer.
- Once you've left, expect your child to stay in bed and go to sleep.
- If your child uses a comforter (e.g. dummy, bottle, nightlight) wean him/her off it as soon as possible. The longer it's used, the more difficult it will be to remove.
- If your child gets out of bed, don't reward him/her with attention. Silently return him/her to bed, and leave immediately.
- Ensure everyone who puts your child to bed sticks to the routine.

Further reading

For a range of ways of soothing a baby to sleep: Sarah Woodhouse, *Sound Sleep: Calming and Helping your Baby or Child to Sleep* (Hawthorn Press, 2003).

Information on brain development: Norbert and Elinore Herschowitz, *A Good Start in Life: Understanding your Child's Brain and Behaviour from Birth to Age Six* (Dana Books, 2004).

For tips on sleep problems: Dr Tanya Byron and Sacha Baveystock, *Little Angels: The Essential Guide to Transforming your Family Life and Having More Fun with your Children* (BBC Books, 2005).

Useful websites

For wide-ranging information on sleep, including a 'caffeine counter' for food and drink: US National Sleep Foundation: www.sleepfoundation.org

The National Sleep Foundation also has a 'Sleep for Kids' site: www.sleepforkids.org

SleepNet (everything you ever wanted to know about sleep but were too tired to ask): www.sleepnet.com/children2000.html

Sarah Woodhouse (see above) has also invented a contraption called the *Bednest* for young babies. It clips on to the side of your bed, so the baby is able to sleep safely beside you – excellent for breastfeeding mothers: www.bednest.com

3. Family Life

Detoxing diet and sleep habits are two obvious ways to establish an authoritative parenting style. You can then extend this to everything that happens at home. The wheels of family life run much more smoothly when children know:

- they're loved (lots of hugs, cuddles and compliments help with this)
- they're respected and their views will be listened to
- their parents enjoy their company and want to spend time with them

- they're looked after (with caring parents firmly in control)
- what their parents expect of them, including clear behavioural boundaries
- what to expect from their parents (regularity and routines help them feel secure)

The left-hand column relates to warmth, the right-hand to firmness. It's much easier to be warm with children in an organised, well-regulated home, so consistent rules and routines are important. In a busy 21st-century home, with so many comings, goings and disruptions, they're more important than ever.

Setting the boundaries

Before you can teach behavioural boundaries, you have to decide what they are. In most homes there are agreed rules covering

- safety, health and hygiene
- social behaviour such as table manners
- morality (Thou shalt take turns; Thou shalt not hit thy sister, etc.)
- simple practices to ease the running of the household, such as putting toys away or not eating before meals.

Then remember that children learn through imitation and repetition. If you want them to put their knife and fork together at the end of a meal, put yours together; if you want them to be polite to the babysitter, model politeness to babysitters. Over and over again ...

To begin with, the adults in charge should decide household rules and routines. As children grow older, they too can help. The idea is gradually to hand over responsibility for behaviour to your child, so they are 'self-regulating' by the time they reach the teenage years.

The tips on the opposite page are only starting points. If you have trouble disciplining your child, it's well worth joining a parenting group, such as Positive Parenting (see page 47). The sooner you do this, the sooner you'll be able to really enjoy your child's company and the sweeter home life will be.

Home sweet home

Home should be a pleasant place to relax for both parents and children. But many adults today feel they must always be rushing about *doing* something. So home becomes somewhere to rush through the chores and collapse in front of the TV. Children often live at a frantic pace too, and are so used to the bells and whistles of electronic entertainment that real life is 'boring'.

Detoxing Behaviour

Be warm:

- Explain (or with older children negotiate) family rules for behaviour and talk about them – why they're necessary, how they'll affect behaviour, etc.

- Always listen to your child's point of view, take it into account and be prepared to change rules to accommodate good points they make.

- If your child breaks the rules, make your initial reaction one of surprise and sorrow rather than anger – indeed, try never to get angry at all.

- Explain what's upsetting you, and how you'd prefer your child to behave.

- If your child is merely testing the boundaries, try to ignore or distract him/her rather than letting the situation escalate.

- Accept that all children fall from grace sometimes. Though you must make your displeasure felt, forgive quickly.

- Praise your child for good behaviour, making it clear what the good behaviour is, e.g. 'Well done – you've tidied everything away perfectly! The bedroom looks great, and you'll be able to find your stuff easily when you need it.'

Be firm:

- Decide with other adults in charge (and older children) on rules for behaviour in the home – perhaps post them up in the kitchen for reference. Remember that adults must abide by them too.

- But don't get drawn into pointless arguments. Make it clear that, in the final analysis, what you say goes.

- But if the behaviour is clearly unacceptable, nip it firmly in the bud – don't let it escalate.

- But if your child doesn't comply immediately, make it clear that you're very displeased, state exactly what you want to happen and insist that it does.

- But never ignore boundary-testing once your child is aware you've noticed; this just encourages them to see how far they can push you.

- But if you threaten or promise something, *always* follow through. Broken promises mean your child won't take you seriously in the future.

- So be very careful about what you threaten. Have some sanctions worked out, e.g. deprivation of pocket money or treats; 'time out' in a quiet part of the house; extra household chores.

One mum of twins said, 'I know I should look forward to the boys' bathtime - it should be a lovely time. But I'm so busy and so wound up - sometimes I just want to drown them!'

Another mother told me about the day she'd tried cooking with her children. 'They were bored from the start, because it took so long to get the ingredients and weigh them. Then the stirring made their arms ache. And when I said it'd take 20 minutes to cook, that was it. I realised that on TV it all happens in about five minutes - they cut out all the boring bits.'

Another advantage of family routines is that they relegate a lot of the day-to-day boring stuff to habit, so everyone just gets on and does it with minimum fuss. For instance, without an established morning routine, getting children ready for school can deteriorate into chaos, a terrible start to everyone's day. But with a routine that runs like clockwork – everyone knows the ropes, no arguing, no messing – the whole family gets off to a much happier start!

Family time, not 'quality time'

One of the most pernicious myths of recent decades is the myth of 'quality time' – those odd snatched hours with one's children, when everyone's supposed to be on best behaviour, 'enjoying quality interaction'. But this isn't how close family relationships work – children aren't like business acquaintances or casual dates, who can be slotted into a busy diary. Although special outings and occasions such as 'family viewing night' (see page 131) are great fun, it's more important just to spend day-by-day time together, hanging out in the same place, following family routines and rituals, getting on with household chores or enjoying a hobby.

These are the times when you can communicate freely with your child, letting conversation develop naturally from whatever's going on. It's also the time when you pass on skills and leisure interests to the next generation. Your child is, in a way, your apprentice – by watching as you do daily tasks such as making a cup of tea, checking email or enjoying a hobby such as fishing or sewing, he or she learns life skills and life enhancement. If, as soon as possible, you let your child have a go, and give lots of praise for effort, your knowledge will soon be passed on.

Some of the skills you teach can eventually become your child's responsibilities in the home. Seen like this, they are less like chores and more like a valued contribution from a family member who is now growing up. The list on page 43 illustrates the sort of life skills children acquire just by being with interested adults. If you don't spend time together, how will they learn them?

Forging a family

The simple truth emerging from this chapter is that if children are to grow up happy and resilient, they need love, time and attention from the significant adults in their lives. Those adults don't need to be parents – they could be grandparents or other relatives, nannies, childminders or other hired help – but the care on offer does have to be loving and consistent, and the adults have to be happy spending time with the child in their care.

Another simple truth has emerged from human history: the best institution for providing loving care is the family. So whether you look after your child yourself, or find other carers for some of the time, you need to forge a strong family base to offer protection against the many risk factors inherent in 21st-century life.

There are many different sorts of family in modern Britain, but whoever the adults in charge, they must be able to spend time with their children, and not just so-called 'quality time'. For many families, struggling to maintain 21st-century lifestyles, this has become increasingly difficult.

Family-friendly work, or work-friendly families?

Work-life balance is one of those thorny issues that worry us so much we're often reluctant to confront it: 'I'll think about it next week,' we think. 'I'm too busy at the moment.' But as an internet philosopher put it, 'If you died next week, the company you work for would fill your place within a week or so. Your family would miss you for ever.' Parents have to find ways of sorting out this problem that they're confident will work for their own family – otherwise, guilt inevitably follows ... and guilt is a very bad basis for human relationships.

Slow down and smell the roses

From the many conversations I've had over the last year, it seems one of the greatest challenges for 21st-century mothers and fathers is to slow down so they can actually enjoy their home and children. Our culture now attaches little status to child-rearing and family life, except in terms of constantly striving for a better lifestyle and more possessions. In a competitive consumer culture running at electric speed, it's difficult to adjust to slow, natural, human rhythms. But it's worth making the effort, not just for our children's sake, but for our own health and happiness. As one father pointed out to me, it's more important to have a life than a lifestyle.

Life skills for a child to learn by the age of 12

When you have to do one of the following chores, invite your child to 'help' – let him or her watch as you demonstrate, then have a go. Give plenty of praise for effort and progress. Next time it crops up, invite your child to help again, and this time do a little more. Give lots more praise. Eventually, you can hand over the task. But don't rush at it – it's not a race – and don't get impatient if your child takes a long time to acquire the skill. Just enjoy the opportunity to spend time together.

Sew on a button	Use a vacuum cleaner
Handwash clothes	Use a potato peeler
Iron a shirt	Clean and dress a wound
Unblock a sink	Use public transport
Wash a car	Find the way home (with map)
Use the phone book	Go shopping (with a list)
Make a hot drink	Mow a lawn
Defrost a fridge	Clean a cooker hob
Change a fuse	Put out the rubbish
Clean a window	Stack and empty a dishwasher
Cook a meal	Take phone messages
Change a plug	Make conversation with a guest
Grow a plant	Use a screwdriver
Change the bed	Give simple first aid (e.g. grazes, burns)
Look after a pet	Check the car's oil and water
Weed a garden	Use a washing machine
Change a light bulb	Contact the emergency services
Sort the recycling	Wash the dishes

And, of course, 21st-century life skills, such as:

Check out a website	Find snail mail details on the internet
Tidy up a desktop	Get rid of spam
Send a text	Download a tune or program

Electric speed versus 'slow time'

It's not just work and general busyness that make it difficult to provide family time. It's our modern mindset. Today's parents grew up in an era of labour-saving devices; we're used to pressing a switch or turning a dial and getting what we want straight away, no messing. At work we're used to multi-tasking – clicking between programs and websites, fielding phone calls and emails, juggling a dozen mental tasks at once.

Not surprisingly, people raised in such a quick-fix world find it difficult to slow down to the much more primitive pace needed for looking after a baby or small child. (I remember comparing looking after a small baby to driving in first gear, *all day*.) For adults used to living at electric speed, it takes an effort of will to slow down to the biological speed required for child-rearing.

But if parents find a way of switching their brains to 'slow time' when with their children, they can start enjoying family time rather than feeling constantly rushed, irritated and exhausted. A mother in Kent told me: 'When I go and pick up the children now I pause before I get out of the car and I say to myself, 'Now slow down, think little people and think slow as you are now going into slow time,' and it really helps me to adjust my mindset from my busy day to that of the children.'

'A tired parent flees a world of unresolved quarrels and unwashed laundry for the reliable orderliness, harmony and managed cheer of work. The emotional magnets beneath home and workplace are in the process of being reversed.'

Professor Arlie Russell Hochschild, sociologist

Detoxing the work-family balance

Be warm with yourself:

- Recognise the supreme importance of **time** in bringing up children – the younger the child, the more 'slow time' you need. Then enjoy the opportunity to escape from the demands of 'electric speed' to the slower, more human tempo of child-rearing.
- Readjust your expectations of yourself (one mother suggests 'Tell yourself you're a hero if you manage to achieve just one thing in a day!').
- If you work, devise a way of moving from work mode into family mode, e.g.
  - ★ use a familiar form of words ('I am now entering slow time')
  - ★ use a boundary, such as getting into the car or opening your front door, when you step from one persona to the other
  - ★ change your clothes – but make sure your 'parent outfit' is one that feels both comfortable and attractive.
- Break free from the traditional view of low-status nurturing and high-status breadwinning. Rearing children is one of the most important things you'll ever do – enjoy it.

Be firm with yourself:

- If you aren't spending enough time with your family, look for ways of changing work patterns. Think about (or preferably discuss with other adults-in-charge):
  - ★ your **real** financial needs (i.e. living costs, as opposed to lifestyle choices)
  - ★ the real effects on career(s) of adjusting the balance, versus the effects on your live(s) and relationships
  - ★ possible flexible working arrangements, e.g. part-time work, job-sharing, working from home, shift-sharing.
- Switch off the computer and put your mobile and phone on answerphone when sharing time with your family. Set times when you will check email and phone messages, and stick to them.
- Force yourself to keep work and family separate, and don't let work-based stress overflow into family time.
- Resist the urge to multi-task at home. For instance, don't have the TV on when you're sharing meals – concentrate on the real-life interaction going on round the table.

Detoxing family life

Be warm with your child and yourself:

- Use the suggestions on page 45 to value family 'slow time', rather than feeling you have to constantly function at 'electric speed'.
- As soon as they're old enough, share hobbies/activities such as gardening, swimming or cycling with children. Family activities are much more valuable than endless clubs and classes.
- Involve your child in the day-to-day activities listed on page 43, and in other household chores. Look on these as opportunities to share 'slow time' with your child, rather than trying to rush through them as quickly as possible.
- Share TV programmes, websites, board games, card games and activities like jigsaws as a family – with each family member taking turns to decide what you'll play.
- Use all these occasions to chat, and also to *listen* to your child.
- If you have several children, every week spend one-on-one time with each. Even sitting outside the school/swimming pool/etc. while another child does an activity is valuable chatting time. So is time together in the car.

Be firm with your child and yourself:

- Expect everyone to stick to family rules and routines (e.g. morning, mealtimes, bedtime) – no deviation, except in very special circumstances. If you are rigid about these things for a while, they will soon become habitual.
- As soon as children are old enough, give them responsibility for simple family chores, such as setting the table or emptying the dishwasher; and expect these to be carried out.
- Expect your child to be punctual and to put household items away after use (and model this yourself).
- Insist on turn-taking, good manners and patience while waiting for others, and model these too. This means recognising that children often take *ages* to complete simple tasks, and being patient when they are 'helping' you.
- Insist on a tidy bedroom from the beginning – I know from bitter experience that if you let this slip, it is very difficult to retrieve it!
- Don't nag – if you want something done, insist it's done immediately. Stand over your child as s/he does it, if necessary.
- And remember always keep to your promises and carry out your threats.

Give yourself regular time off from both work and child-rearing, and if you have a partner, reserve some special time each week to spend together. Children benefit hugely from spending some time with other adults who know and love them, especially grandparents.

Further reading

Margot Sunderland, *The Science of Parenting* (Dorling Kindersley, 2006).

Mary Pipher, *The Shelter of Each Other: Rebuilding our Families* (Ballantine Books, New York, 1997).

Carl Honore, *In Praise of Slow: How a Worldwide Movement is Challenging the Cult of Speed* (Orion, 2004).

Ros Kane, *To Have an Only Child* (Do It Yourself Press, 2005).

Jane Whittingstall, *The Good Granny Guide* (Short Books, 2005).

Flora McEvedy, *The Step-Parents' Parachute: The Four Cornerstones to Good Step-parenting* (Time Warner, 2005).

Useful websites

Raising Kids: www.raisingkids.co.uk

Parents Online: www.parents.org.uk (magazine format)

Family Onwards: www.familyonwards.com (magazine format, particularly good on divorce, second families, etc)

Parentline Plus: www.parentlineplus.org.uk (national charity, information plus a network of parent volunteers offering help and advice to other parents)

MumsNet: www.mumsnet.com (UK-based information and community network for mothers)

Fathers Direct: (National Information Centre on Fatherhood) www.fathersdirect.com

Dads and Daughters: www.dadsanddaughters.org (US organisation)

Positive Parenting: www.parenting.org.uk

4. Playtime

Perhaps the most serious change in children's lifestyles over the last twenty years has been in habits of play. Now that endless entertainment is available at the touch of a button, it's all to easy for screen-based activities to take over from real-life experience. Television, computer games and electronic chat are addictive; before you know it, there's no time for anything else. But play is essential for young human beings – you can see from page 51 how it underpins every aspect of development. From their earliest years, children need opportunities for active play, especially outdoors and with other children.

However, as well as electronic entertainment, there's another obstacle to genuine play: consumerism. Manufacturers have created a huge range of toys, and marketeers spend millions of pounds selling them to children. But the more expensive the toy, the less children tend to play with it. Real play is creative and imaginative. We have to provide the conditions for children to move from toy consumption to genuine play.

Getting off to a creative start

Children are programmed to play creatively, so all parents have to do is provide safe environments (inside and outside) and a few inexpensive props. These suggestions come from the child development experts I consulted for *Toxic Childhood*:

- Collect interesting but safe items (e.g. wooden spoons, large pine cones and shells, crackly packaging, discarded lids or boxes, bits of fabric, ribbon or fur) and keep in a basket or box that your child can rummage in and select from.
- Share picture books and TV programmes with your child – this provides lots of ideas for play.
- Let your toddler experiment with basic objects, e.g.
  - ⋆ a large empty box can become a car, boat, space rocket . . .
  - ⋆ a cloth or sheet can become a den, a bed for teddies, a costume . . .
  - ⋆ pots and pans can be filled and emptied, banged to make music, piled up, knocked down, carried about . . .
- Choose a place for messy play – preferably outdoors – and on different occasions provide sand, water, mud, paint, bubbles, clay, cooking ingredients, snow ... Give your child sticks and spoons for mixing and containers for filling and emptying, and stay close by on safety watch.

Don't feel you have to provide something different every day. Young children like familiarity, so are happy to return to the same activities time and again. Indeed, repetition of these early play activities helps create strong neural networks that will support later learning and creativity.

Detoxing creative play for all ages

Be warm:

- Let children of all ages carry on messing with the stuff listed above.
- Share books and TV programmes and see what ideas they inspire.
- Provide areas, indoors and out, where your child can set up a house, castle, shop, garage, vet's . . . (Let children take playthings outdoors as often as possible.)

Be firm with your child and yourself:

- Limit the time your child is allowed to spend on screen-based entertainment.
- Make it clear you aren't impressed by toy consumption. Allow some coveted items for Christmas and birthday presents, but if your child wants anything else, they can save up for it.

- Encourage your child to make models and props for imaginative play from junk, boxes, etc.
- Create a dressing-up box full of old clothes, hats, fabric, ribbon, beads (second-hand shops yield some great dressing-up clothes).
- Encourage den-making, indoors (cloth over a table?) and outside (cloth over branches for a wigwam?).
- Provide paper, paint, crayons, pens, glue, glitter, etc. for making greetings cards, posters for family events, albums, books ...
- Buy a cat litter tray and encourage your child to make 'small worlds' (farms, islands, alien planets) or use boxes stuck together to make a dolls' house.
- Go out collecting – leaves, stones, shells, cones, insects, worms, tadpoles. If it's alive, look after it and watch it grow.
- Listen to music – move to it, or try making it with anything around.
- Let your child make mixtures and potions in bottles and jars, using stuff from kitchen, bathroom, garden, etc. (but remember safety precautions).
- When the weather's good, provide the ingredients for outdoor water play – a bucket or large bowl of water is enough.
- Give plenty of praise for your child's artistic creations, and put some on display.

- When children take playthings outdoors, insist that *they* bring them back inside when play is over.
- Always insist that all toys and equipment are put away after a period of play. This means letting children know that time's up well in advance of the deadline. It also means having simple, readily accessible storage systems.
- Train your child to handle potentially dangerous items, like scissors, appropriately and don't brook any messing about.
- When providing materials for children's play/cooking/making, always do a quick risk assessment first. Explain any safety precautions carefully, ensure children understand and insist they follow them.
- Don't feel you always have to provide play ideas. Leave your child to play alone or with friends. When you do join in with your child's play, don't take over – stand back! If you always direct operations, they won't learn to figure things out for themselves.
- If children take toys or other equipment outdoors for water play, insist they wash them (this can in itself be fun) when play is over.
- Don't expect the things they make to look good – it's the making that counts, not the product.

What do **you** remember?

When I work with parents, I ask them to spend a few minutes remembering how they played when they were kids. It's fascinating to watch their conversations – people become very animated, and there's always a lot of laughter. Then I ask for a show of hands on how many of those memories were of outdoor play. Almost always, among parents of twenty or older, it's a full house.

Only a generation ago, it was normal for children to go out to play, and to wander more or less unsupervised around their local area. The parents I speak to often go all misty-eyed, and say, 'We'd just go off down the park/to the woods/to the pond, and our mums had no idea what we were doing!' or 'We'd be off on our bikes for hours on end and only come back when we were hungry.'

The everyday play experiences of today's children are very different. This is the first time in human history that children en masse have been reared in captivity – and we don't yet know how this change of lifestyle is going to affect them in the long term.

What children learn from outdoor play

Play is one of the main ways we learn and yet, when we reach adulthood, we tend to forget all about it. It's like a ladder children climb towards adult understanding, and as soon as we've climbed it we kick it away. So most adults have forgotten what they learned as they roamed freely around their local area. It probably included:

- common-sense understanding of the world and how it works (the properties of water, mud, wood, sand and so on; the effects of friction, leverage, etc.)
- risk assessment (including judging distances, testing boundaries, learning who and what to trust)
- social skills (making friends, turn-taking, sorting out difficulties, how to get along, organising and cooperating)
- self-reliance and control (getting lost/found, coping with minor injuries/accidents/disappointments)
- the pleasure of doing, making, creating, imagining (dens, forts, ships, houses – pretend-play of all kinds).

When we keep children cooped up indoors, they miss out on these vital lessons. You can't learn these skills second-hand from a screen – you can only learn them through first-hand real-life experiences.

Some recent research findings:

- Today's three-year-olds are as sedentary as office workers.
- An 11-year-old's common-sense understanding of how the world works is two to three years behind that of children 15 years ago.
- The area of official playground space available for each child in the UK is about the size of a kitchen table.

How free-range children have become battery kids

So why have parents suddenly started keeping their children indoors? As usual, there's a complex mix of reasons.

- A huge increase in traffic makes many areas dangerous for children.
- The availability of seductive indoor entertainment means children no longer have to be under their parents' feet when indoors.
- Now most people have cars, we're far less used to being outside – we've become wimpish about the rain, scared of getting cancer from the sun, worried by the thought of having to walk any distance.
- Most insidious of all, over the last 20 years there's been a huge growth in adult anxiety about children's safety, leading to fierce over-protectiveness.

The causes of parental paranoia

The 21st-century plague of adult anxiety is a result of our technological culture. News – often very unsettling news – is now beamed into homes in all its realistic glory 24 hours a day. Scientists have found that when people repeatedly view disturbing images, it changes the way they think.

Lifelike pictures (such as modern TV images) bypass the logical centres of the brain and go straight to the emotional centres. So instead of thinking logically about what we're seeing, we have a more primitive, immediate, emotional response.

We see graphic and prolonged coverage of child abduction,
and we think: PROTECT!
We see terrorist atrocities like the Beslan siege,
and we think: PROTECT!
We see natural disasters tearing families apart,
and we think: PROTECT!

Even though parents *know* that the chances of these things happening to our family are millions to one, we don't think logically. Our brain reacts to the TV coverage as if the threat we see is right outside our door. Psychologists found that people who repeatedly viewed the Twin Towers disaster suffered the same symptoms of post-traumatic stress as people who were actually there.

Advertisers, media moguls and politicians play on these fears. They know that fear sells stuff and wins votes. Since the coverage goes on all day long, they've helped convince us that the world is infinitely dangerous.

From battery kids to free-range children

In fact, the greatest danger to 21st-century children is parental over-protectiveness, which now threatens every aspect of their development. This is one of the most pressing social problems of our time, and it will require the full force of parent power (see page 147) to solve. But the suggestions on pages 57–58, culled from a variety of experts, are a good start.

Peeling the potatoes off the couch

Sports clubs and other organised activities are one way of getting children out and about, and boys particularly benefit from competitive team games (although not *too* competitive – it should be fun).

But children also need opportunities to play out in an unstructured way, without too much adult supervision. This is how they learn independence, self-control and social skills, essential if they are eventually to be self-regulating teenagers and adults.

This means finding safe places they can play, and ensuring that there's just enough supervision to keep them safe, but not so much that their independence is threatened. One way to do this is to make contact with other local parents and arrange to 'keep an eye out' for all the children in your neighbourhood (see page 148).

A teacher told me about two little boys, six and eight, whose parents ran a pub. It was on a busy corner so the children were never let out to play – they were being raised like battery chickens in a room over the pub. Both boys had behavioural problems at school and the older one seemed to be dyslexic – the outlook for their educational future looked poor.

Then the parents changed their jobs and moved – to a house across the road from a playground. The children began to play out every day. Within weeks, their behavioural difficulties had disappeared and after a couple of months the eight-year-old was reading on schedule. Their futures now look bright.

It can be difficult to uproot your couch potatoes if you've lost confidence in their ability to play outside. One mother told me that her children complained about being 'booted outside' on a Sunday morning, instead of playing on the computer or games console, or watching a video. 'It was only because I now know how important outdoor play is that I was able to insist. But when you tell them firmly that they're going out, and that's that, it's amazing how long they'll play happily at making mud pies, building camps and so on. I just needed the confidence to overcome their initial resistance.'

Another mum was concerned that there was no big open space for her two young sons to play locally. 'But then we went for a walk and found this little patch of wasteland with a couple of trees and a slope. It didn't look particularly promising to me, but the boys loved it. They spent most of the afternoon just rolling a ball down the slope and scampering down to get it. Over and over again. I suddenly realised that outdoor play doesn't need to be complicated.'

And as a father in Kent put it: 'There are advantages to encouraging children to play out. Outside they find it easier to sort out their own disputes and find their own solutions to problems – like using a stick as a stirrer or a lever or a prop. It develops their initiative and their independence, which means the adults have more time to get on with household chores.'

The age at which children are ready to play out without adult supervision varies from child to child. It will also be affected by the area you live in, the proximity of safe playing spaces, and many other considerations. This is one of those decisions that only a parent can make. But the more family time you've spent introducing life skills and demonstrating safety procedures, the more confident you'll feel that your child is ready for more independence. And if you've encouraged loosely supervised outdoor play (in the garden, for instance, or with you at the park) and seen him or her gaining in initiative and common sense, that will increase your confidence too.

My mother was determined to make us independent. When I was four years old, she stopped the car a few miles from our house and made me find my own way home across the fields. I got hopelessly lost.

Sir Richard Branson, founder of the Virgin empire

Education outdoors

We also need to make sure that children in schools, preschools and 'extended schools' have opportunities for outdoor loosely supervised play. Over the last decade, the shameful tendency of local authorities (encouraged by government) to sell off school playing fields means there are far fewer open spaces now attached to urban schools.

But playing fields are by no means the only sort of outdoor spaces children need. Young children naturally seek out enclosed, sheltered outdoor spaces. Evolution has wired them to enjoy making dens and scrambling through undergrowth, much safer places in prehistoric times than the open plains. Yet schools seldom offer this type of outdoor play space – just wide open tracts of mowed fields and tarmacked playground.

In 2006 an outdoor nursery opened in Hampshire (www.farleynurseryschool. com), where children can play outdoors in all weathers in the wide open spaces. The day I visited, there was a huge pile of gravel to play with, logs to walk along, an area for messing about with water, a large mud-pie section, fields for running, and the makings of a treehouse. (Children could also play indoors if they wanted, but most preferred to be outside, appropriately wrapped up for the weather.) The school's been praised by school inspectors – Ofsted has marked it as 'outstanding', explaining that 'the children thrive in a stimulating and vibrant environment'.

But even in the middle of the city it's possible to create exciting outdoor play spaces for young children. The Chelsea Open Air Nursery is just off the King's Road in London, and in a space no bigger than a decently sized suburban garden the staff have created a magical play area, with sand, water, mud, dens, trees, hiding places and performance space.

In 2007, a nursery where children play outdoors all day opened in Scotland ('The Secret Garden', Monimail Tower, Fife), based on the 'forest schools' in Scandinavia. Its headteacher says: 'It's adults who create a negative attitude about the weather. Someone told me in Norway there's no such thing as bad weather ... you've just got to have the right clothes.'

Detoxing the great outdoors

Be warm:

- Spend time outdoors with your child, helping him or her become streetwise and safety conscious. Walk together to school, daycare, the shops and so on. Demonstrate road safety procedures and praise your child for following the rules. The more you do this together, the more confident you'll feel about your child's competence.

- On your travels, look out for safe places where your child and friends can play outside, such as parks, your own or neighbours' gardens, recreation grounds and school fields, local 'wild places', or on the pavement outside home if the street's generally free of traffic.

- Take your child to play in these places, and make sure they know how to stay safe there.

- Go for 'expeditions' with your child in the local area, work out safe routes and spot shops, public buildings etc., where your child could go for help in an emergency.

- Ride with your child on local buses, trams and trains rather than taking the car. Demonstrate how to use local transport and understand the routes.

- When you feel your child's sensible enough to go out to play with

Be firm with your child and yourself:

- Reduce anxiety levels by watching less TV news, and don't tune in to repeated re-runs of unsettling news. Read it rather than watch it.

- Don't have the news on during the day when children might watch it.

- Work hard to resist irrational fears, and balance worries about letting your child play out with the knowledge of how important outdoor play is.

- When introducing your child to the great outdoors, make yourself go out in bad weather as well as good, dressing appropriately. Children need to experience all sorts of weather and if you model wimpishness, they'll learn it.

- Be very firm about teaching road safety rules, stranger danger, etc. Insist that your child repeats the rules as you explain them and learns them by heart. Revise the rules regularly.

- Ensure your child knows how to tell the time. Buy him/her a watch and insist on good timekeeping, explaining that lateness is worrying for parents.

- If your child is late back after playing out, ground him or her for a while. Make it clear you won't tolerate bad time-keeping.

friends, give him or her a mobile phone (to be used only in emergencies) or tracking device, so you can keep tabs on where they are.

- Encourage interest in outdoor sports and if possible enrol your child in sports clubs (but avoid excessively competitive sport for the under-12s).
- Turn up to cheer your child on in sporting events, but don't get over-competitive yourself.

- Insist your child always lets you know where they're off to and who they're playing with.
- Insist also they check with you or another trusted adult if there's a change of plan.
- Make all safety procedures such a routine that they wouldn't dream of forgetting. And if they do, read the riot act and make sure they realise how much upset they've caused.

Of course, occasionally accidents happen. Like parents through the ages, we just have to make risk assessments, skill our children in safety procedures and then keep reminding ourselves how vital to their development freedom to play is.

Actually, no matter how hard we try to remove risk, accidents *will* happen – so there's no point in losing sleep about them. All we can do is pray that the only accidents affecting our children will be minor ones, and useful learning experiences.

Further reading

For ideas for creative play for young children:

Diane Rich, Denise Casanova et al, *First Hand Experience: What Matters to Children* (Rich Learning Opportunities, 2005).

For ideas for outdoor play:

Fiona Danks and Jo Schofield, *Nature's Playground: Activities, Crafts and Games to Encourage Children to get Outdoors* (Frances Lincoln, 2006).

Con and Hal Iggulden, *The Dangerous Book for Boys* (HarperCollins, 2006).

For more information about the causes of and remedies for parental anxiety:

Tim Gill, *No Fear: Growing up in a Risk-averse Society* (Calouste Gulbenkian Foundation, 2007).

Richard Louv, *Last Child in the Woods: Saving our Kids from Nature-deficit Disorder* (Algonquin Books, 2005).

For information about the importance of physical play and movement:

Sally Goddard Blythe, *The Well Balanced Child* (Hawthorn Books).

Useful websites

General information about play, with many useful links: Children's Play Council: www.ncb.org.uk/cpc/

Ideas for creating safer streets: www.homezonenews.co.uk

Great ideas for play spaces: www.freeplaynetwork.org.uk

How to improve school grounds: Learning through Landscapes UK www.ltl.org.uk

Information about play in the London area: www.londonplay.org.uk

Section II

Detoxing Childcare and Education

What's Wrong With Childcare?

Until about twenty years ago, most people were pretty clear where childcare ended and education began. Childcare happened at home and was the responsibility of the family; education happened at school and was up to the teachers. But as more mothers started going out to work and childcare turned into an industry, the lines have become increasingly blurred.

- Many young children today are cared for in an institution (such as daycare nurseries) for many hours a day, rather than at home.
- Extended schools (childcare facilities on school premises before and after the school day) mean that some six- to twelve-year-olds spend very little time at home at all.

What's more, the idea has recently taken root that daycare and pre-school are mainly a preparation for school, rather than a separate stage in growing up. So the 'childcare' aspect of looking after children gets emphasised less and less. In fact, many people have begun to think of it as little more than babysitting.

Yet bringing up children is not the same as babysitting. The suggestions for detoxing parenthood in the last chapter – and the ones to come – are not something you can do in your spare time. Caring for children is serious, important work.

Learning versus education

Caring for children *does* involve helping them to learn, but not in a formal school-like way. The learning is quite natural and springs from everyday activities and chat, the sort of thing described on pages 78 and 87. And it's very much rooted in the love and attention of the parent or adult in charge.

This sort of learning begins the moment a child is born. Babies learn about the world around them, the people in it, and about themselves, as they gradually gain control over their bodies. Within a year or so, they're learning to walk and talk. Once they have the freedom of movement and the tools of language, their learning takes on another lease of life.

And it all happens naturally, because the child *wants* to do it. Children learn through natural curiosity, through imitation and repetition, and through play (if you think about it, most play is imitation and/or repetition). Adults don't *teach* them to sit up, crawl, walk or talk – just help them learn by giving attention, support and praise.

On the other hand, social graces – like toilet training, saying please and thank you, and following family rules – often do need some teaching. So do skills like washing and dressing oneself, using cutlery, and all the life skills listed on page 45. But most of us wouldn't consider this sort of teaching to be 'education'. It happens naturally as part of *care* – the care of loving adults giving the child time. For healthy development, childcare of this sort should be seen as an end in itself, not as an add-on to education.

Attachment and communication

As well as keeping their charge safe, sheltered and well fed, the adults who care for a child have a huge impact on the sort of person that child eventually turns out to be. We've seen in Section I how bringing up a child requires a great deal of time and attention – establishing habits and behaviour, providing real food, real play and real first-hand experiences.

Good childcare, whether provided at home or elsewhere, must cover all these areas. And it must also provide for attachment and language development.

Attachment is the scientific name for the deep bond between a child and the person who cares for it. It is particularly important in the first year or so of life, when the 'attachment figure' is usually the baby's mother (although it doesn't have to be).

As time goes on, children also form attachment bonds with other loving adults. A child's personality, behaviour and learning are all rooted in secure attachment. In later life, a child who's securely attached will usually find it easy to form strong relationships. It's also a key factor in long-term emotional resilience.

Language skills grow out of the same deep bond between carer and child. When a mother talks, sings and plays with her baby, she provides the baby with data about language. Gradually the child begins to make sense of this 'mother tongue' and, eventually, to copy it. Throughout childhood, children learn new words and ideas through chatting and sharing experiences with the adults who care for them. These communication skills are vital for children's social and cognitive growth development.

Who do you remember?

In the talks I do for parents, I sometimes ask them to remember one person from their childhood who was very special to them. Overwhelmingly, they remember someone from their family or a close family friend. And when I ask why this person was important, the response is always that they had *time*. Time to listen, time to share, time to tell stories, time for all the activities described in the 'be warm' sections throughout Chapter One.

This is what children need most from the significant adults in their lives: time. When beloved adults spend time with them, children feel cared for and secure. But in a fast-moving, multi-tasking society, time is often the one thing we can't spare.

Why don't we value childcare?

If time with loving adults is so important for children, we have to find some way of providing it. But so far, as a society, we haven't really grasped this nettle. We've recognised the importance of education, but not of care. Indeed, childcare workers, whose job is basically to spend time with children, are among the lowest-paid workers in the country.

The reason, of course, is that childcare has such low status. Throughout history, it's always been 'women's work', done at home along with the cooking and cleaning. In the past, rich mothers often palmed it off on to a nanny; even if they would have liked to look after their children themselves, it was thought to be 'beneath them'. Poorer working mothers usually left their children with female relatives – grandmothers, aunts, elder sisters, who looked after them unpaid.

As women gained equality over the 20th century, they wanted the same status as men. It was clear that, in a man's world, status (along with financial independence) could only come from paid work outside the home. So women too began to see childcare as low status, and often looked down on stay-at-home mothers who decided not to go out to work. But it's now becoming clear how important that 'women's work' is. Our lack of respect for the business of caring for children is a key ingredient in toxic childhood syndrome.

Consumer values and childcare

Our booming consumer culture has added to the toxic brew. In a competitive world, parents are understandably anxious to give children a head start. They're happy to invest money in their children's future but since they don't see the significance of childcare, they spend it elsewhere.

- Wealthy parents pay a fortune for private school fees, extra-curricular clubs and classes. But rather than 'wasting' time or money on childcare, they often go for the babysitting option – a young au pair, who knows nothing about raising children, and spends most of her time on the phone to her boyfriend.

- Parents who can't afford school fees look for other ways to improve their children's chances, including forking out for expensive electronic equipment, in the belief that it's educational. (It has the added advantage of keeping their child 'safely' cocooned in a virtual world, while they work long hours to afford more consumer must-haves.) But they can't imagine throwing away their cash on something as low status as childcare.

In fact, good-quality care, especially in the first few years, is probably the most significant investment any parent can make for their child's future. As shown throughout this book, it creates firm foundations – emotional, social and cognitive – for that child's growth through life.

Childcare, education and communication

The rest of this section looks at childcare and educational needs during three stages of development:

- birth to three
- three to six
- six to twelve.

In each stage, I pay special attention to the growth of children's language, since this underpins much of their future development:

- **emotional** – children who can speak up for themselves and express their needs are more self-confident and resilient
- **social** – good language skills are an essential part of getting along with other people
- **cognitive** – all school-based learning relies on spoken language skills, especially learning to read and write.

Children who can communicate well are likely to grow up bright, balanced and able to take full advantage of their education. So it's important that the people who look after them have time to talk and listen. Alongside love and attention, talking and listening are perhaps the most vital factors in good-quality childcare.

In a 2006 report, the communications charity I CAN found a clear link between poor language development on starting school, school failure, anti social behaviour and youth crime. A survey the next year by the same charity showed that parents spend less time chatting with their children than watching TV and doing household chores.

1. Birth to Three

What do babies and toddlers need?

During their first three years, children need full-time one-on-one care. As always, this involves a balance of warmth and firmness:

- love, time and individual attention to ensure that all the child's needs are met
- routines, rituals and rules to provide security and safety.

This is the time when sleeping and eating habits are laid down, when family routines are established, and when – in a loving home – the child develops that deep sense of security that underpins future resilience.

Clearly this involves the constant time and interest of a loving adult. This is usually the mother, but it doesn't have to be. It could be a grandparent or a paid minder. These days, many fathers heroically stay the course. So I'll talk about the 'mother-figure'.

The importance of attachment

The mother-figure is a child's first and most important attachment figure. Over the first six to nine months, s/he should be a constant, consistent loving presence in the child's life. Children who are secure in this first relationship easily form attachments to other people –

family members, nursery workers, and so on. In later life, they'll continue to find it easy to form strong relationships. Even so, in the first couple of years, there shouldn't be too many people involved. Small infants don't cope well with change, so too many new faces are unsettling.

Attachment needs at different ages

0–6/9 months	6/9 months–2 years	2–3 years
For secure attachment a baby needs a constant and consistent mother-figure. Others can help, but the less the baby is separated from the mother-figure, the better. Care should be home-based. Institutional care at this age should be avoided.	A child who is securely attached should by now be happy to spend a couple of hours a day away from the mother-figure. But too many changes of carer can still be damaging, and home-based care is preferable to institutional care.	Securely attached children should by now enjoy spending time with other children and will probably thrive in a nursery for several hours a day. But they still need the security of plenty of time spent with the mother-figure, in a familiar domestic environment.

The mother-figure options are:

- Mum, Dad or another family member (youthful enough to cater for the needs of a baby or toddler)
- a nanny (expensive but usually highly qualified)
- a childminder (less expensive, and in her home rather than yours, but usually good-quality care)
- a named key-worker in a day nursery providing care in a home-like environment.

The problems of institutional care

The first three of the options listed at the foot of page 69 consist of one-on-one personal care. The final one is an attempt to provide this one-on-one care in an institutional setting.

While day nurseries are often convenient, it's much more difficult to ensure secure attachment for children through institutional care. Even though there may be a named key-worker to act as 'mother-figure', the chances of her being consistently available are less than in any of the personal childcare scenarios.

As the childcare industry has mushroomed in recent years, there are increasing questions about the quality of care on offer:

- Carers may be poorly qualified and poorly paid – some may simply not know how to talk, play and interact warmly with the children, especially if they haven't been particularly well parented themselves.
- There may be a high turnover of staff, which interferes with attachment.
- There's often a lot of bureaucracy, so time may be spent on ticking boxes rather than with the children.
- Owing to new government regulations, carers may be encouraged to chase educational targets rather than to give love and attention.

> One nursery nurse who has to write two progress notes on each child every day told me: 'I'll be playing with a child and having a great time, but then I'll think – "Hang on a minute, I'll have to write that down!" And then the moment's gone!'

Having now spent two years researching this topic, visiting day nurseries and talking to parents and childcare workers, my advice would be to look at all the other options first. Personal one-on-one care is more likely to fulfil the needs of a baby or toddler than care in an institution.

Don't try to go it alone!

Personal one-on-one care in the first couple of years offers the best chance of good attachment for the child, but it can cause problems for the mother-figure. In our splintered 21st-century communities, mums, dads and others caring for very young children often find themselves spending days at a time with no adult company. A complete lack of social life is difficult for anyone, but especially for people who've previously been used to the social buzz of the workplace.

So it's important to get out and about, and find other people in the same boat with whom to build mutual support systems. Babies need daily fresh air too, and to mix with other babies to play (and also to build up immunity to childhood illnesses).

If you plan to look after your own baby, you can start making these contacts before the baby's born, perhaps through joining an organisation like the National Childbirth Trust or checking out websites such as those listed on page 75 – but don't get drawn into too much web-based socialising or use it as a substitute for real life. Real-life social contacts help you interact more with your baby, but too many screen-based activities stop you communicating and can interfere with attachment.

Once children are a little older, it's usually easy to find local mother and toddler groups and so on. But more important than organised meetings are opportunities to spend ordinary domestic time with other parents – perhaps sharing a shopping trip, making and eating a meal together, or taking your children out for a regular stroll in the park. These are the human contacts that lead to collaboration and genuine support.

Handing over the baby

If you aren't able to look after your child yourself, but still want one-on-one care, the obvious solution is to employ someone else to take your place. A live-in nanny may cost too much for most parents to contemplate, but childminders are often no more expensive than a nursery place. Many child development experts now believe a childminder may be the best alternative to parental care, especially in the first few years.

But even then, the care of a much-loved infant is never straightforward. Parents sometimes find themselves struggling with jealousy when their child becomes attached to someone else. So it's really important that you get along with the person you choose, and that you're prepared to share your child's affections with her. You also have to share attitudes to child-rearing and agree on all the rules and routines outlined in Section I – the transition between parent and minder should be as seamless as possible.

And then there's the question of trust. Some parents I interviewed said that, in the end, they chose a day nursery rather than a childminder because at least in a nursery there's built-in supervision. There's no one to watch what happens when you leave your child in a minder's home.

The best of both worlds?

A charity in Soho has come up with a way of combining the one-on-one care of a childminder with the supervision of a nursery, while at the same time offering the minders some adult company and support. It offers a base where a dozen childminders can work together. Each childminder looks after up to three children (only one of whom is a baby) and is paid directly by the children's parents. But the childminders bring their children to the centre during the day.

This means they can share some chores (such as nappy-changing or cooking meals) while still remaining the mother-figure to their children. The older children can play together, and the childminders can benefit from each other's company. A childcare supervisor, paid by the charity, ensures the effective running of the centre. Perhaps something like this is the 21st-century way forward for early childcare outside the home?

Detoxing childcare

Be warm with yourself:

- If you want to look after your baby, do everything you can to do so. Forget about lifestyle and instead enjoy **life** watching your baby grow into a toddler.
- Remember that a change of job (or even career) as a result of taking a few years out is not necessarily a bad thing.
- Make contact with other parents and build up a social support network so that you're not isolated and depressed.
- If you decide not to look after your child yourself, don't beat yourself up. Look for the best possible one-on-one care.
- Make sure you get on really well with whoever you choose to look after your child.

Be firm with yourself:

- Accept that having a child will make a significant difference to lifestyle, whether you care for the child yourself or pay someone else.
- Accept that decent childcare costs money – if you don't want to do it yourself, buy the best care you possibly can.
- Plan carefully so that you avoid chopping and changing arrangements, especially in the first couple of years.
- Accept that if you hand over the role of 'mother-figure' to another person, you might find it hard. Don't let jealousy spoil your relationship with whoever you choose to look after your child.

Further reading

Steve Biddulph, *Raising Babies* (Harper Thorsons, 2006).
Sue Gerhardt, *Why Love Matters* (Brunner-Routledge, 2004).
Sally Goddard Blyth, *What Babies Really Need* (Hawthorn Press, 2007).

Websites:

Information about attachment: from What About The Children? (WATCh?)
    – www.whataboutthechildren.org.uk
For meeting other parents: e.g. National Childbirth Trust www.nct.org.uk,
    www.meetmums.co.uk or www.mama.co.uk
Information on childcare options: e.g. the Daycare Trust
    www.daycaretrust.org.uk; National Network for Childcare
    www.nncc.org; Child Care Link www.childcarelink.gov.uk

Starting to communicate

Communication starts the moment a mother looks into her newborn
baby's eyes. At first it's just smiles, coos and body language from
Mum and uncontrolled burbling from the baby. But babies learn
through imitation and repetition, and the natural behaviour of adults
when caring for babies provides many opportunities for both.

Babies are born able to speak any language on earth. They learn
their 'mother-tongue' from listening to the adults who care for them:

- First they recognise the sounds of the language – adults help them
  with this by talking to babies in a simple exaggerated, rhythmic
  way known as 'parentese'. They tend to repeat the same phrases
  time and again.
- Gradually children begin to imitate repeated sounds in their own
  babble.
- Gradually also they start to recognise words, as adults talk about
  what's going on around them: 'Look at the doggy. Isn't he a lovely
  doggy?' A familiar homely setting means plenty of opportunity for
  repetition of key words.
- As time goes on and children gain increasing control of their lips,
  tongue and vocal chords, they utter their own first words.

The power of song

The traditional songs and rhymes that have been used to comfort and entertain babies and toddlers through the ages are important in many ways. For a young baby, a gentle rocking rhythm associated with the mother's voice is soothing – a comforting routine, laying down the first patterns and pathways in the brain. As time goes on, it's vital to language development because songs and rhymes

- emphasise the sounds of language – **B**ye **b**aby Bunting; **D**ance to your **D**addy; **R**ing-a-**r**ing-a-**r**oses
- provide plenty of repetition – songs and rhymes can be pleasurably repeated hundreds (maybe thousands) of times
- are easy to imitate – once the child has begun to master language, s/he can begin to join in, and so practise making the sounds in an enjoyable, soothing way.

But as well as helping with spoken language, this gentle 'tuning in to sound' lays solid foundations for reading and writing, when children have to 'decode' words from their sounds (**c-a-t** makes cat).

Language development

Age	Type of talk	Examples
0 – 1	– babble – early attempts at words around one year	*Dada*

1 to 2	– more recognisable words
	– lots of repeated words
	– around 18 months puts
	   two words together
	– uses question intonation
	– by 18 months, knows up
	   to 50 words, by two years
	   up to 200
		Bye-bye
		Oggy-oggy
		Mummy sleep?
		words for actions, food,
		body parts, clothes,
		animals, vehicles, places,
		colour, shape

	– by two, 2/3 words together in short sentences – starts using question words	*That my house* *What that noise?*
to 3	– puts 3/4/more-word sentences together – possibly 500 words by 2; 1,000 by 3 – asks endless questions – uses *and* to link ideas	*Me got lotsa cars like Tom.* *Daddy comed to see me* *in the garden* *Why? Why? Why?* *I want juice and bikky!*

Why electronic babysitters don't work

Television, video or computer programmes cannot be a substitute for human beings in these early years – a key part of early communication is eye contact, cuddles and smiles. And words only make sense to very young children when they're part of a real-life context that they can see, touch and understand. So, at this stage electronic entertainment probably does much more harm than good.

- It can't truly interact with the child, so the language young children hear on screens is largely meaningless to them.
- It can fascinate children, distracting them from interacting with real people.
- It can distract adults from interacting with their children – many carers now watch TV, do the email or listen to an iPod while nursing a child, instead of making eye contact and singing or chatting.
- It can be used as a substitute for naps (keeping children absorbed and apparently resting), which is dangerous because napping time is important for learning (see page 32).

Here's looking at you, kid

It's amazing how many ways technology comes between adults and very young children. Another recent invention that interferes with communication is the forward-facing buggy. In the 1970s, as car-ownership began to soar, there was a demand for lightweight buggies that could be folded up and put in the boot. The best design for a cheap, safe, folding buggy was one where the baby faced the same way as the pusher. Ever since, almost all buggies have faced outwards – and parents believe it's more interesting for children to see where they're going.

But from the point of view of both attachment and communication, child and adult need to be able both to make eye contact and to see the same things. It's a communication triangle:

- The child looks out at the world, then checks back to the adult.
- The adult looks to where the child's been looking and responds – for instance: 'Oh, what a lovely doggy!'
- The child is reassured that all is safe, enjoys the shared experience and begins to associate the word 'doggy' with the creature s/he's seen.

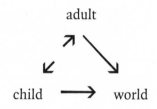

Dummying down

All young children cling to comforters of various kinds, and since it's instinctive for babies to suck, most find dummies particularly comforting. But in order to learn to talk, children need practice. First they need to babble, to get used to making the language sounds; later they need to practise talking. If the baby's mouth is filled with a dummy, this practice doesn't happen. Dummies should therefore be used with discretion, and children weaned off them as early as possible.

Detoxing communication

Be warm:

- Talk to your baby or toddler as often as possible – when you're out and about and as you do household chores. Make eye contact, smile and, if you can't think of anything to say, just give a running commentary on whatever you're doing. Don't worry that your child can't understand.
- If you point something out, make sure your child can see where you're pointing. Remember the communication triangle on the previous page.
- Whenever you have time, sing nursery songs and lullabies, recite nursery rhymes, and use repetitive games like Patacake, tickling rhymes and number chants – and encourage your child to join in.
- Encourage your child to start 'conversations' (whether it's odd words or just body language) and respond to each communication.
- Tell stories and read to your child; children love to hear the same story again and again.
- When your child starts to speak, repeat and expand the words. For instance 'Mummy cup' – 'Oh yes, mummy can get you the cup.'
- Listen carefully when your toddler speaks and always try to respond in some way.

Be firm with yourself:

- Turn off the TV, CDs, computer, etc. when you're with your child. Concentrate on him/her instead.
- When sharing time with your child, stop yourself from rushing and multi-tasking. Slow down to more 'human' pace.
- Don't rush a child who is trying to communicate with you, and don't look away.
- Try also to minimise interruptions from communications technology. Switch off the mobile, switch the phone to answer machine, resist the temptation to check the email – you would do this for an important person at work, and who is more important than your child?
- Make sure that when you're communicating with your baby or toddler, s/he can see your face. Buy a buggy that allows your child to face you.
- Don't ever think of talk with your child as 'educational'. If you try to educate, it'll stop being fun and it won't work.
- Be firm about retaining regular ring-fenced 'family time', such as mealtimes, shared activities, bedtime, when there's plenty of space for talk. Don't let these be eroded by busyness.

- If your child says something incorrectly, don't point out the mistake. Just say it back the right way.
- Praise your child for using new words correctly.
- Encourage your child to talk to other adults or children (translate if their language is unclear, but don't talk for them).
- Try to 'open up' your child's language by listening carefully and asking genuine questions.

- Don't let under-twos watch much TV. Limit TV for older children, and keep to shows designed for the age group.
- When your child begins to watch TV, watch with him or her as often as possible and talk about the programmes.
- Don't 'close down' your child's language by asking teacherish closed questions (to which there's one right answer).
- Never criticise or make fun of the way your child speaks.

Further reading

Professor James Law/ Johnson & Johnson, *Learning to Talk: A Practical Guide for Parents* (Dorling Kindersley, 2004).
Dr Richard C. Woolfson, *Small Talk: From First Gestures to Simple Sentences* (Hamlyn, 2002).

Useful websites

The Talk To Your Baby campaign covers early language and attachment www.talktoyourbaby.org.uk
The communications charity I CAN provides information on language development and speech problems: www.talkingpoint.org.uk

2. Three to Six

What is quality preschool?

By the time they're three, most children are ready for several hours a day of child-centred, play-based, preschool learning. Good preschool education starts from children's own interests and caters for all aspects of their development, not just the cognitive. As well as child-centred learning, there are activities organised by the teacher, such as singing and moving to music, and a regular storytime to help children settle into a larger social group.

At this age there are great differences between children's levels of development, especially between the sexes. Boys tend to lag behind girls in terms of language, social skills and the ability to sit still or do small, fiddly tasks. Girls may show a much earlier interest than boys in reading and writing, but be less interested in how things work, and less confident in outdoor physical activities. A good preschool encourages children's natural interests (it would be just as wrong to hold a child back as to push him/her to achieve before s/he's ready), but also broadens their horizons.

Moving into learning

All learning starts in movement. Children need to explore their world to understand it. They need physical coordination and control before they can sit in a classroom and listen quietly to a teacher. And they need good hand-eye coordination in order to read and write.

Physical coordination tends to develop earlier in girls than in boys, so girls often seem ready for schoolwork a good year or so before their male counterparts. Boys usually need far more opportunities to run, jump, climb and engage in rough-and-tumble play before they're ready for formal learning. Their slower language development means they also take longer to pick up spoken language skills, and need more structured opportunities for doing so.

But girls need time to move and play too. Just because many are happy to make an early start on reading and writing doesn't mean they should bypass the types of large-scale (often outdoor) play that lead to physical confidence and competence. Girls often need encouragement to run about, jump, climb and develop spatial awareness and risk-taking skills. Without opportunities to do so, they may end up timid and risk-averse.

Learning to read

Parents are understandably anxious about their children learning to read, so when their offspring are three or four they often want to press on and make an early start. But if children aren't ready to read (and boys particularly are often far from ready at this age) starting formal teaching too soon can do more harm than good.

The luckiest children learn to read 'naturally' by the 'Read Aloud, Read Along, Read Alone' method:

- Beloved adults read favourite books aloud, lots of times.
- The child starts joining in, reading along with repeated or favourite lines.
- With lots of enjoyable repetitions, the child gradually starts 'reading' books alone.

Of course, initially the child is just reciting from memory, but over time begins to associate the shapes on the page with the words, and that's the start of real reading.

To read fluently, children also need to learn phonics (c-a-t spells *cat*). If they've had plenty of exposure to language (especially songs and rhymes – see page 76), many children pick this up quite quickly. It also helps to look at alphabet books together, to have an alphabet frieze up in the bedroom and to sing an alphabet song.

But otherwise, my advice as a literacy expert is to leave the actual teaching of phonics to school. While phonics teaching was out of fashion for many years (leading to widespread reading failure), it's now firmly back on the primary school timetable. If you teach your child phonics beforehand, s/he's going to be very bored having to go through it all again.

The best way parents can help is to introduce children to the joy of reading – and to give them a 'reading habit'. You'll do that by sharing and talking about books together, and reading aloud to your child every day, even after they've started reading for themselves.

Too much too soon?

Over the course of two or three years of good preschool education, the teacher directs more and more of the children's activities, gradually laying the foundations for more formal schoolwork (including a playful introduction to phonics). In most European countries formal learning doesn't start till children are six years old – in fact, in the countries with the best educational record (Sweden and Finland) children don't start to read, write or do written sums until they are seven. But in England in recent years there's been a tendency to start on the 3Rs ever earlier – at five, four or even three – largely due to a political obsession with tests and targets.*

★   Wales and Northern Ireland have begun to adjust their early years curriculum to be more like the European model, and there are glimmerings of similar changes in Scotland. It's England that's obsessed with a early start to formal education.

It's important to resist this 'too much too soon' mentality (see Parent Power, page 142). Research is clear that, for long-term success at school, three- to six-year-olds need to be actively engaged, thinking and talking about their first-hand experiences. Often this talk arises between children as part of their play, but they also need opportunities to talk with adults to increase their vocabulary and understanding of the world.

Even if your child is 'academic', rushing into a more formal curriculum is unlikely to increase his or her chances of success. The many lessons to be learned through play (see pages 48-51) are greatly enhanced by the structured play opportunities available at a good preschool. It may look as though children are just messing about with sand, water, paint or clay, but they're actually learning – through first-hand experiences – about the properties of materials. Later, when they study physics, this deep understanding will be important. Similarly, playing in the role-play corner with other children teaches social and communication skills . . . and even the most academic of children need to be able to get along with other people.

Children are not brains on legs: they're whole human beings and we need to pay just as much attention to their physical, emotional, social and conceptual development as we do to formal, cognitive learning.

> Research published in 2006 showed today's 11-year-olds are two to three years behind their 1990 counterparts on tests of conceptual development – that's the common-sense understanding of the world that underpins scientific knowledge. This is an alarming finding, as without conceptual understanding, children find it more difficult to learn and remember. It was during those 15 years that outdoor play seriously declined and early education became increasingly formal.

Juggling education and care

Three- to four-year-olds benefit from about three hours per day of preschool, and for four- to six-year-olds this can be up to six hours per day. But they all still need childcare around the edges of preschool education. And if you work, it's still a question of choosing between personal and institutional care.

Personal care

Part-time attendance at a preschool, with some kind of personal one-on-one childcare around the edges.

The options for providing personal care are:

- one or both parents reduce working hours to allow for childcare, e.g. part-time work, job-sharing
- one or both parents adapt work to fit around childcare, e.g. shift work, working from home (this can put stress on individuals or partnerships)
- a nanny, child minder, family member or unqualified helper, such as an au pair, to cover when you aren't there.

Institutional care

Full-time care in a day nursery where educational activities are mixed with 'family-like' mealtimes, rests, play and so on. Full-time nursery may seem the easiest option, but it can also be effortful in terms of:

- arrangements for dropping off and collecting children
- keeping in touch with carers to ensure your child is happy
- any parental duties expected by the nursery (as one mother put it: 'You're usually required to keep up your end of the grunt work, regardless of whether you work outside the home.')
- dealing with emergencies, e.g travel arrangements breaking down.

Keeping the balls in the air

Whatever you choose, remember that you need a steady routine with as little chopping and changing as possible. So:

- put in plenty of groundwork on providing the best possible option from the beginning
- devise efficient emergency systems, including more than one trusty 'safety net' should your arrangements go awry.

Detoxing childcare and education

The points made on page 74 still apply. In addition:

Be warm with your child and yourself:

- Make sure your child has plenty of opportunities to explore and learn and the chance to meet and play with other children – several hours a day at preschool should provide this. But remember the importance of loosely supervised, unstructured play (see pages 48-56).
- Read to your child, and share favourite books over and over again (see page 82).
- Encourage counting rhymes and songs, and games that involve counting – first to ten, then to twenty and so on.
- Share music (not just pop music) with your child – if your child shows an interest in music, encourage it.
- Give plenty of opportunities to paint, crayon, model and construct with a variety of materials.
- Make sure your child has lots of opportunities for creative play indoors and out (see pages 47-50).
- Remember that young children *want* to learn. Unless we turn off their interest by pushing them towards activities they're not yet ready to tackle (or by letting them sit getting square eyeballs), they'll make progress.

Be firm with your child and yourself:

- In choosing a preschool, think about your child's long-term developmental needs (physical, emotional, social and conceptual as well as cognitive).
- Ensure there is also plenty of family-type care around the edges of learning opportunities.
- Avoid frequent changes of childcare arrangements.
- Don't push your child to learn at this stage. Let the child's interests lead the learning, rather than adults always deciding what they should do.
- Don't try to push your child to read before s/he shows an interest in doing so. Once interest develops, encourage and support your child, but keep it fun.
- Encourage music, but don't push your child to learn an instrument unless s/he shows an interest. If s/he does, explain that, if you pay for a series of lessons, you'll expect your child to stick to them throughout the course.
- Don't think of 'education' as more important than 'play' – in the years up to six, children learn most of the important lessons through enjoyable, child-friendly, first-hand experiences.

Carry on communicating

These are great years for children's language and learning. They're fascinated by the world around them and now they can talk about it, their thoughts and imaginations can soar. So keep talking, listening, thinking and wondering.

To develop children's thinking skills, talk should be open-ended. Avoid asking questions to which there's only one 'right answer' (e.g. 'What is that shape called?') and don't worry if you don't know the answer to questions yourself. Instead, encourage your child to come up with his or her own ideas and explanations. You can worry about 'right answers' later – in the early years, it's more important to encourage active, creative thinking.

Planning
Let's think about what we/you are going to do. What will you need? Tell me how you'll start. Gosh! What will you do then?

Wondering
I wonder what this is? What d'you think that's for? I wonder how it works? Any idea where this should go? Look! What's going on here? Why d'you think that happened?

Remembering
Can you remember what happened when ... ? Where were you? Tell me how it all started. What happened next? How did that feel?

Predicting
Can you guess what will happen next? What do you think would happen if we ... ? (or if we didn't...?)

'What shall we talk about?'

Some starting points if you're feeling tongue-tied:

Early morning talk

- 'So, what's going to happen today?'
- 'What's the weather like? How will it affect our day?'
- 'Which clothes to wear today?' (and why they're right).
- Talk your child through how to do things (e.g. tying a bow: 'First you make a loop, and pinch it with your fingers. Then you wind the other lace round ...')
- Lots of praise as your child gets better at organising and dressing.

Family time talk

- Family stories ('Do you remember when ... ?')
- Household objects (what they're for, where you got them, how they work).
- Children's feelings ('How did you feel when....?')
- Favourite TV programmes (e.g.'What did you think of the way so-and-so behaved?')
- Advertisements, and how advertisers try to influence you.

Mealtime talk

- Talk through the events of the day (e.g. 'Tell dad about what happened on the way home from school.')
- Tell other adults about your child's achievements that day.
- Plan/discuss the evening to come, or the next day's events.
- Talk about the food: where it comes from, what it tastes like, why it's good for you.
- Talk through table manners, how to eat certain foods, etc.
- Praise for eating up, good behaviour, etc

Bedtime talk

- 'What was the best part of your day?' 'What's happening tomorrow?'
- Bathtime talk and play.
- Talk through bedtime rituals (e.g. teeth-cleaning, putting clothes away) – repetition of the same forms of words helps embed routines.
- Praise your child as s/he learns to do things independently.
- Tell or read a story.
- Your goodnight ritual – use the same form of words each night.

Shop talk

- Make shopping lists together (talk about choices, plan meals).
- Ask your child to help as you shop ('Can you find the beans? I need two large tins.')
- Chat about where you go, what you see, why you choose one item rather than another.
- Negotiate behaviour ('If you do so-and-so, you can choose a comic at the end.')
- Plenty of praise for good behaviour.

Kitchen talk

- Talk about ingredients for meals (what they're made of, where they come from, what they taste/smell/feel like, and what you do to them, e.g. weigh, chop, mix, slice, grill, boil) .
- Wonder about changes that happen to the food, e.g. shape, colour, smell, texture and taste at different stages.
- Go off at tangents, e.g. 'I wonder why onions make us cry? What sort of food might make us laugh?'

Outdoor talk

- Chat (or make up stories) about what you see: people, animals, places, etc.
- Talk about the weather, how trees etc. change with the seasons
- Talk through rules for road safety, stranger danger, etc.
- Make up games (e.g. 'Let's make up names for the people we see.' 'How many white vans can we spot between here and home?')
- Praise your child for safety knowledge and sensible behaviour.

Car talk

- Sing and recite rhymes together.
- Play memory games (e.g. 'Mrs Brown went to town and she bought a . . .' players take turns to recite the list, adding a new item).
- Plan or talk through events of the day (e.g. 'What was the best thing that happened today?')

You've got a captive audience in the car, so it's a good time to bring up issues you need to talk over, or gently encourage your child to 'open up' about anything that's bothering him/her.

Trips down memory lane

All children love hearing stories about themselves and their families:

- things they used to do 'when they were little'
- stories about parents' and grandparents' childhoods
- family tales and anecdotes.

It helps develop a strong sense of their identity and their place in the world. Often they enjoy hearing the same old stories time and time again. So if you're at a loose end, get out the photo albums and videotapes and indulge in some reminiscence.

Further reading

Ros Bayley and Lynn Broadbent, *How to Help your Young Child to Succeed* (Network Continuum, 2006).

Ros Bayley and Lynn Broadbent, *Flying Start to Literacy* (Network Continuum, 2007).

Diane Rich and others, *First-hand Experience – What Matters to Children* (Rich Learning Opportunities, 2005)

Useful websites

Talk to Me! campaign on www.basic-skills.org.uk
Information about quality preschool: www.early-education.org.uk

The dumbing down of the nation's children

In 2005 local councils in the UK tested the spoken language of children entering primary schools. In many parts of the country, they found more than 50 per cent of children had language delay. One disadvantaged area found that 84 per cent of the children were seriously behind in speech development. This is a severe and growing problem.

3. Six to Twelve

The best days of their lives

Once they start school, children are legally required to spend up to seven hours a day there, so the 'childcare time' around the edges is greatly reduced. But primary pupils are still children, and still developing. Now that so much of their lives is spent away from home in an institution, parents have to be confident about what happens to them there.

Over the last five years, I've asked many thousands of parents, teachers and children what they think primary education is for. Their answer always boils down to three main points:

- to teach children the 3Rs, on which all other education depends
- to encourage children's interest in learning, so that they go on to secondary school bright-eyed, bushy-tailed and ready to make the most of their talents (whatever these might be)
- to help children get along with each other and adjust to the rules and routines of educational life.

If parents agree with this wish list, they need to be sure that the primary school their child attends is suitable to fulfil it.

What's wrong with primary education?

Most parents are broadly happy with their child's primary school, but there are some widespread concerns:

- are standards high enough?
- why is there so much bad behaviour and bullying?
- why is my child bored?

As a close observer of the primary educational system for thirty years, I believe there are three main reasons behind this unease.

Too much too soon

First of all, we try to rush our children to achieve too early. Changes to the school admissions policy in the 1990s mean that most English children start formal schooling at four – two or three years earlier than children in most other European countries. This early start is particularly damaging for boys, most of whom are simply not ready to cope with formal learning (see pages 81-82), and is probably leading to lower standards of attainment overall, rather than raising them.

Winners and losers

Secondly, there's the problem of pressure: England has the highest number of exams and assessments in the world. Starting when children are six or seven years old, primary education is dominated by high-stakes tests and targets. Children therefore learn very early in life whether they are winners or losers. The losers often give up trying (and contribute to the behaviour/bullying problem), while the winners face the stress of 'staying on top' for the whole of their childhood and adolescence.

The learning turn-off

Thirdly, the primary curriculum is overloaded with academic 'teaching objectives' – in fact, it's little more than a watered-down secondary curriculum. Along with heavy emphasis on the 3Rs (to ensure 'high standards' in the tests) this dull, dry learning often turns children off, rather than inspiring them to learn more. Interestingly, the schools that get the best results are those where the headteacher is brave enough to ignore government guidelines, and aim for a more exciting, creative approach.

England has the worst record in all three areas, but other countries in the UK have similar problems. It's not surprising that many primary schools have difficulties with behaviour, that many of the children who *can* read actually hate doing so, and that once they reach secondary school we have one of the highest drop-out rates in the world.

> A headteacher in Kent spoke for thousands of teachers I've met over the last few years: 'When I started teaching 20 years ago I had 40 children in my class and no teaching assistant, but children weren't kicking off like they do now. They were much more able to monitor themselves and self-regulate.'

It takes a village ...

As the problems of primary education escalated over the last couple of decades, parents have voted with their feet. Those who can afford it opt for independent prep schools, where they know their children will mix with others of similar social status, and probably have a better chance of long-term success. In the state sector, there's intense competition to get children into 'good schools'. These tend to score well in the annual league tables, largely because they too draw on more privileged catchments. Thus the gap between the educational haves and have-nots grows worse every year.

Here's part of an email from a father in north London:

'In a relaxed, non-pressured way, parents want to get their kids into the best schools at primary and secondary level, and they face a highly competitive situation. Obviously, the broad political point is that our schools need to get better as a whole . . . but what parents want is clear advice on how to help their children do the best they can on a personal level . . . Parents hate themselves for competitive parenting, but it's hard to break the cycle, especially when the competition isn't just local but national as well.'

Clear advice in these circumstances is not easy to give, but for what it's worth, this is mine:

- I wouldn't call it 'competitive parenting' to do everything possible to get your child into a school you feel confident about. Just make sure your tactics aren't themselves likely to damage your child's development. (Parents who engage tutors for their three-year-olds or send children to hot-housing nurseries probably do much more harm in the long term than good.) Sending a beloved child to a primary school you don't approve of would just make you feel guilty and unhappy, a bad basis for family life. But when choosing a school, do remember the detoxing tips on page 99.

- If you can't find such a school in your local area, there are alternatives, all costly in either time or money:
  - ⋆ look further afield – perhaps move house, perhaps think about paying
  - ⋆ educate your child yourself at home (see www.educationotherwise.co.uk)
  - ⋆ look into alternative schooling, for instance the Steiner Schools (www.steinerwaldorf.org.uk), which base education on children's all-round development (while fee-paying, they try to keep costs down, drawing instead on parents' expertise)
  - ⋆ get together with other parents and set up your own school –

this isn't as mad as it sounds (indeed, it's how many of the Steiner Schools started).

If you have ideological qualms about deserting the state system you can always carry on working for political change from outside.

- But if you're lucky enough to find an acceptable local school, don't assume you can hand over responsibility for your child and sit back. Schools need support to rise above the tide of tests, targets and bureaucracy. Work with staff and other parents on projects and campaigns to benefit your child *and other children*. Many parents today see other children as irrelevant (or as competition), but in primary school your child is learning to be part of a social group, and for one to thrive, all must thrive.

- If parents – bright, articulate parents who have benefited from education themselves – work with their local school in this way, they might start nudging the system in the right direction (see Parent Power, page 142).

> In the same week as that father's email, I received this note, from a mother in south London: 'Don't ask "What is the school doing for me?" but "What can I do for the school?" Schools need intelligent, motivated, capable people to run clubs and extra-curricular activities and it's amazing, when you start asking around, just how many skilled and capable parents there are out there – artists, musicians, interior designers, food specialists, linguists … We have a lovely psychologist in our street who's almost permanently engaged by the local school, helping children with behavioural and cognitive disorders (all for free).'

If, like the south London mother and her philanthropic neighbour, parents became more involved in their children's education – running clubs, working on the PTA, offering help in the classroom – primary schools could become a central point of contact for everyone interested in detoxing childhood.

This sort of involvement would take up precious time, of course . . . but then, successful child-rearing is time-consuming. It's also collaborative, social, and draws deeply on parents' personal strengths and their relationships with others in the community. In the words of a justly famous African proverb, 'It takes a village to raise a child.'

A village; not a state.

Parents versus teachers

But while the primary school system is crying out for an injection of informed Parent Power (see page 142 onwards), after 20 years' battering by government and media, individual school staff may not be entirely welcoming. Morale in education, as in all the public services, is at an all-time low. In the teachers' loo in a Liverpool school, I saw a poster that sums it up pretty well: 'The flogging will continue until morale improves.'

In a winners and losers educational system, parents and teachers are often at odds. The competitive system makes them distrustful of each other, and keen to offload blame whenever possible.

'Teachers and parents come from different corners, and have different goals. Parents want red-carpet treatment for their children; teachers want to keep their classroom show on the road. Parents get frustrated when schools don't take them seriously; schools get hostile and defensive when parents make demands they think unreasonable.'

Hilary Wilce, educational agony aunt, Independent

Before we can detox childhood, we need to detox the relationship between school and home. This involves both sides accepting responsibilities:

- Schools need to be welcoming to parents, to keep them well-informed, to consult them and genuinely take their opinions into account.
- Parents need to know and follow school procedures, keep up to date with information, ensure they're doing their bit towards their children's development, and maintain good contacts with the school.

- Teachers and parents need to be honest with each other about what they want for children (and, in the final analysis, this is more likely to be the wish list on page 91 than a narrowing of the curriculum, and endless coaching and 'boosting' to get the school's required quota of 'levels' in the Key Stage 2 SATs).

So parents have to choose a school carefully (not on league table results, but on whether it feels right for their child), support it as much as they possibly can, and work on the assumption that they and the teachers are on the same side.

File it!

When your child starts primary school, put the prospectus and other information into a loose-leaf binder and keep this somewhere handy. You then can add other school correspondence, such as

- notes and newsletters with term dates, staff changes, new procedures, etc.
- your child's school reports, special commendations or certificates
- correspondence between you and the school.

Keeping a folder like this means that you – and everyone who looks after your child – can easily keep up to date with information about the school's organisational ropes. This gets you Brownie points.

If something goes wrong

If something does go wrong for your child at school try, as usual, to respond with a balance of warmth and firmness.

- First of all help your child talk it through. Try to work out what's actually happened, and see if s/he can find a way to deal with it (see page 102).
- If your child is in trouble (with a teacher or another child), look at both sides of the argument – don't automatically leap to his or her defence. Loving your child doesn't mean assuming s/he can do no wrong.

- On the other hand, no one knows your child, or cares about his/her welfare, as much as you. If you believe the other party is in the wrong, you must act.
- If the problem is a long-term one, start a log. Make a brief dated note of everything that happens; it's easy to forget incidents or mix up times, and that weakens your case.
- Don't rush in to complain in an angry or upset state of mind. Keep calm and use the correct channels to put your point of view (this is where the folder comes into its own). Don't be tempted to go 'straight to the top' as this can escalate problems rather than solving them.
- Check who to contact in your school folder and write a letter about the problem first, keeping it as calm and reasonable as possible. It helps you sort out what's gone on, and you can also be sure the main facts are clearly stated (and that you don't forget any in the heat of the moment). It's also useful if it's necessary to take the case further (i.e. to school governors or county/city authorities).
- Before going to any meetings, think about what outcome you would like – what do you want the school to do to sort out the issue?

Could do better?

Every year more and more children are diagnosed with learning diffi-culties. If your child is one of them, don't despair. As the mother of a dyslexic, I know how soul-searing it is to see your child struggling at school. But the key is to concentrate on their *abilities*, while doing everything you can to support the disabilities. If you can keep their self-esteem going until they're through GCSEs, life will look up again – I promise! Meanwhile, read Noel Janis-Norton's excellent book (see page 104).

Detoxing education

Be warm with yourself, your child and the school:

- Choose a school that encourages the development of the whole child rather than focusing on test results.
- Aim for a friendly and trusting relationship with your child's teacher – remembering there are thirty other children and parents in his/her class.
- Be positive about school when talking to your child – parental attitudes rub off. You want your child to be positive about learning, so:
  - ★ look for things to praise about the school and your child's teacher, and hold your tongue about things that annoy you
  - ★ don't gossip carelessly with other parents in front of children.
- Stop yourself from competing by remembering that children develop at different rates. A child who's doing wonderfully today may slow off tomorrow; a slow starter may eventually overtake everyone.
- As usual, the most important way parents can help children do well is to talk and listen to them (see pages 62-103).

Be firm with yourself, your child and the school:

- Do your homework when choosing a school, e.g. read the prospectus, arrange a visit, chat with other parents in the area.
- Make sure you know the organisational ropes (e.g. expectations about homework, arrangements for taking children to school, collecting them, and so on). Integrate these into family routines so they become second nature.
- Always turn up to parent-teacher interviews. (If you can't make it, write to ask to arrange an appointment another time. Don't expect teachers to be able to stop for a chat about a child without notice.)
- Don't be conned into thinking of primary education as a sort of race. The children who do well in the long run are those who
  - ★ enjoy learning for its own sake, not just to get stars or high marks
  - ★ are motivated to learn and don't give up easily
  - ★ get along with their teacher and other children.

- Give heartfelt praise for your child's achievements, especially evidence of hard work and effort. Show your delight when things go well.
- If you think your child isn't achieving as well as he or she could, don't nag – discuss what's going wrong and look for ways to help.
- Support the PTA, attend meetings and functions. These are a chance to meet teachers informally and get to know the parents of your child's classmates.
- Take every opportunity to bond with the parents of your child's friends, but beware of school gate gossip – rumours and misunderstandings easily get out of hand. The best policy is 'hear no evil, see no evil, speak no evil'.

- Don't overdo the praise. If you go into raptures about everything your child does, it won't carry much weight when it's really justified.
- Never pile on the pressure if things are going wrong. If your expectations are too high, it can damage your child's chances of success.
- Make sure your child knows what bullying is (and isn't) and how to deal with it, including reporting straight back to you and/or a teacher (see websites on page 104).
- If anything goes wrong at school, control your emotions and try to be as rational and open-minded as possible – see pages 102–103 for strategies.

Juggling education and care

The 'round the edges' childcare choices for school-age children are the same as those for preschoolers (page 85), but children's need for 'home and family time' changes as they get older. On the whole, the younger the child, the more s/he needs the comforts of home around the edges of the school day, but if children are securely attached (see page 69), by the time they're nearing double figures they'll probably want to spend time out and about with friends.

As long as you're happy about the friends, this developing independence is to be encouraged – see pages 51-6. Good childcare in these circumstances means ensuring that the outdoor 'adventures' available to your child are as safe as possible without impeding the development of independence.

Extended schools

So where do 'extended schools' fit into all this? Unfortunately, government didn't design school-based childcare in the best interests of children, but as a way of keeping working parents out feeding the economy. It's basically a very cheap babysitting service – and babysitting isn't the same thing as good childcare.

To fulfil children's needs, extended schools need to act 'in loco parentis'. This means offering the same care I've described so far in this book, especially

- healthy food and family-type mealtimes
- loosely supervised, unstructured play, indoors and out
- opportunities to learn life skills and hobbies from adults
- opportunities for talk with well-known and trusted adults around first-hand experiences.

If these conditions are achieved, and your child is keen to stay on in school around the edges of the school day, then your childcare worries are over. And, with the exercise of parent power and some creative thinking on behalf of government, it probably is possible.

But if you or your child are less than enthusiastic, it would be better to take advantage of the extended school services on no more than one or two days a week, and continue with the sort of childcare provision described on page 85.

Even big kids need families

No matter how old children are, they still need family time. Children continue to need family meals, sensible routines and the sorts of family interactions described on pages 40-46 until well into the teenage years. There's research showing that teenagers who eat with their families are less likely to be involved in drugs or alcohol abuse, have higher self-esteem and, if they're girls, are less likely to get pregnant.

It's still good to talk

The suggestions on pages 88-89 for talking and listening are still appropriate throughout childhood.

School talk

To engage your child in talk about school ask open-ended questions, for instance: 'What was the best thing that happened today, then?' 'Bring me up to date on that story, the one the teacher's reading you.' 'What's this Roman project all about?' The more interest you show, the more you actively listen to their responses, the more children are likely to talk.

Problem talk

If your child has a problem, try these strategies, based on counselling techniques:

- Tune in to the way your child is behaving and by listening and/or watching body language, try to gauge how they're feeling. Describe what you think's going on, e.g. 'You seem really frustrated ... angry ... sad ... today. Are you OK?'
- Don't push it. If your child starts to talk, listen carefully, resisting the impulse to interrupt. If not, keep quiet, give out sympathetic vibes and try again another time.
- When your child talks, acknowledge with nods, 'uh-huhs', and so on, listening carefully. In genuine pauses, try to recap what you've understood: 'So Andy has been really nasty, but you don't understand why? He's saying things to the others, and you're feeling victimised.'
- Don't try to offer solutions. Help your child find them through questions like 'Is there anything you can do?' or 'What are you

planning?' If you think your child's plans might backfire, be subtle: 'How do you think Andy might react to that?' 'Is there any way that could go wrong?'

- Try to listen so sensitively that your child sorts the problem out – then give lots of praise and support for his/her cleverness.

Behaviour talk

As children grow older, the more you can negotiate about behaviour and problems with family rules, the better. Try this simple 'conflict resolution' technique:

- Don't get into an argument. Stay calm. Breathe deeply and think 'Warm but firm, warm but firm!'
- Ask your child to explain his or her point of view. Listen carefully, and don't interrupt.
- Then ask your child to listen to you while you explain your point of view. Be brief and stay polite (even if s/he wasn't!).
- Discuss how you can come to a negotiated settlement. Use the counselling techniques above to help your child make decisions, rather than leaping in and making them yourself.

This is clearly a time-consuming process, but try it, say, once a week. Once you've had some practice, you'll find it gets quicker and easier. And children who can negotiate are at a huge advantage throughout life.

Further reading

Warwick Mansell, *Education by Numbers* (Politicos, 2007).

Hilary Wilce, *Help your Child Succeed at School* (Piatkus, 2004) – very balanced advice from the *Independent's* educational agony aunt.

Noel Janis-Norton, *Could Do Better* (Barrington Stokes, 2005) – an excellent starting point for parents whose children are not thriving in the education system.

Bill Lucas and Alastair Smith, *Help your Child to Succeed: The Essential Guide for Parents* (Network Educational Press, 2002) – good advice on learning in and out of school.

Adele Faber and Elaine Mazlich, *How to Talk so Kids Will Listen and Listen so Kids Will Talk* (Piccadilly Press, 2001) – the bible on how to talk to children and teenagers.

Useful websites

Websites for help with bullying: www.bullying.co.uk; www.kidscape.org.uk; www.parentlineplus.org.uk

Independent advice on a range of educational issues: The Advisory Centre for Education: www.ace-ed.org.uk

Advice on education law: www.childrenslegalcentre.com

The official government website for education in England: www.dfes.gov.uk

Watch this space

In 2006, Professor Robin Alexander began an independent review of primary education in England, the first such review for forty years. He leads a 20-strong panel of the great and good, from within and outside education – but not appointed by government. They'll gather evidence and, eventually (they don't say when) produce a report which will probably bring about significant changes. My book *Toxic Childhood* has been submitted in evidence.

See www.primaryreview.org.uk.

Section III

Detoxing the Electronic Village

'Yeh, yeh, it's just more material for my blog.'

Growing up in an Electronic Village

'It takes a village to raise a child.' As all parents know, the influences on children extend far beyond the family, taking in their friends, neighbours, teachers and all the people they meet on the way through childhood. So, throughout history, parents have relied on other members of the community to help raise their children. And the other adults in the 'village' have risen to the challenge – after all, it's in every villager's interests that the next generation grows up healthy and well adjusted.

Today's children are growing up in a very different sort of village – the 24/7 electronic village of global communication technology. In the last 20 years, technology has made the whole world our oyster. On TV, we can meet *Friends* in New York, *Neighbours* in Melbourne, *Teachers* in London. Via the net, we can forge friendships, swap neighbourly wisdom, and learn from experts around the globe. Wherever we are, we have mobile communication at the touch of a button. The electronic village is full of wonders, with many more wonders to come, and our lives are all much the richer for it.

But like any village, it has its dangers: people living among us who are not what they seem, 'strangers' who might do children harm. While most people living in the global village are genuine friends and neighbours, there are also strangers on screen and online who *can* do harm, not to mention the shadowy army of anonymous manipulators lurking behind the screens.

If our children are to grow up healthy and well adjusted, we must make sure they're safe in the electronic village, just as we would in the real world. In the long term, this may take concerted action by the general public and politicians (see Section IV, page oo). But in the meantime there's plenty parents can do at home to ensure their own children get the best – not the worst – out of our brave new world.

The splinter effect

A nine-year-old boy I met in 2005 told me proudly about his 'virtual world', a high-tech bedroom containing TV, DVD-player, computer, games console and goodness knows what other technological paraphernalia. Apparently he spent almost all his out-of-school hours in there. 'So where are Mum and Dad while you're in your virtual world?' I asked. He thought for a moment. 'Well, Dad's in his virtual world watching the football, and I think Mum's doing the email.'

It sounded terrifyingly familiar. It's a deep irony that the more we can communicate with people around the globe, the less we talk to our nearest and dearest. In how many homes nowadays is each member of the family locked for hours at a time into a personal virtual world, missing out on family time, shared hobbies and the chance just to hang out together and chat?

When I talk about this with parents' groups, everyone begins to look slightly guilty, but everyone agrees that families probably spend less time in each other's company than ever before. 'I blame central heating!' cried one older lady. 'In the olden days, only one room in the house was warm, so everyone had to be in the same place.' She has a point – we've been drifting apart for ages. But I suspect the huge increase in the number of TV channels in the early 1990s was the final nail in the coffin. Parents thought they were being kind when they bought their children TVs to stop the fights over the remote control, but in fact they were splintering their families.

It didn't take marketing men long to recognise that separate TVs for different family members meant they could target their ads much more efficiently. Not surprising TVs suddenly got much cheaper. Now 40 per cent of children under five and 80 per cent of the under-12s have a TV (and a lot of other electronic equipment) in their bedroom.

Children's retreat into a 'virtual world' crops up in every single aspect of toxic childhood syndrome – from the loss of real play to the increase in bad eating habits (the effects of ads plus solitary snacking) to lack of sleep (the electronic equipment fizzing late into the night).

In fact, if I could make one change to modern children's lifestyles it would be to

GET THE TVS
(and all the other electrical stuff)
OUT OF THE BEDROOMS!

The dark side of the village

Apart from anything else, when children watch TV in their rooms, parents don't know what they're watching. You may think your child is plugged harmlessly into CBBC, but children are curious creatures, prone to channel-hopping, and it won't be long before they've found something much more interesting to watch.

In 2000 a number of influential organisations, including the American Medical Association, American Psychological Association and American Academy of Pediatrics, issued a joint statement: 'At this time well over 1,000 studies . . . point overwhelmingly to a causal connection between media violence and aggressive behaviour in children.' Given that children learn through imitation and repetition, and the average American child has by the age of ten witnessed about 100,000 acts of violence and 8,000 murders, this is not exactly surprising.

No action was taken as a result of their statement – nor in response to scores of other studies since, showing exactly the same causal links

– because too many vested interests are involved. Media magnates and marketeers (and the businesses they represent) know violence brings in the punters, so they lend their powerful support to the anti-censorship lobby.

It's the same with sleaze, smut and profanity. As TV companies vie with each other for audiences, there's a constant upping of the ante in terms of sexual content, antisocial behaviour and bad language. The more viewers become accustomed to violence, sex, swear words and generally degrading behaviour, the more difficult it is to shock us, and the more outrageous programmes become.

Someone has to call 'time' on this process. The lowest common denominator of television plumbs lower depths with every passing week. Don't wait for the media to do it; they're locked in competitive combat. And don't rely on politicians, who recognise a can of worms when they see one, and carefully keep out of the argument. It probably has to be parents, because this is stuff that no one wants their child to imitate or repeat.

But so far parents have kept quiet. Some are worried about seeming prudish, old-fashioned or extreme right wing. Others assume that 'someone' must be sorting things out; surely the government wouldn't let anything damaging happen to children? Would it? And almost everyone seems unaware of basic facts about children's emotional and social development.

Violence and other unsavoury aspects of the media *do* influence children's behaviour and emotional stability. We've now had more than a decade's opportunity to watch the effects of growing up in a 24/7 electronic global village, and it's time the grown-ups got together and tackled the toxic effects on their children (see page 149 for information on two mothers who *are* trying to do something).

In researching for *Toxic Childhood*, I came across three major areas of concern:

- increasingly aggressive marketing to children
- the effects of the visual media on children's brains
- the abuse of electronic communications.

Tackling these issues will take concerted action on behalf of parents, the general public and politicians, and there are details of some starting points in the final section of this book (page 148). In the meantime, I urge individual parents to assess the evidence summarised in the following pages and – if they find it as worrying as I do – make lifestyle adjustments for their own children.

Parents who've already detoxed their corner of the electronic village assure me that it isn't just easy; it makes family life much, much more pleasant.

Responsible TV stations could help a lot in the detoxing process. In summer 2007, BBC's *Panorama* ran an experiment where a group of parents removed TV from their homes for a fortnight. Some noted startling improvements in their children's behaviour, and all were astounded at how much more time they had for family life, and the knock-on positive effects that had on their children.

> Perhaps *Panorama*'s call for the whole nation to take up the challenge of reducing children's TV watching signals the beginning of a culture change? It is certainly more in keeping with the BBC's original aim not only to entertain, but to inform and educate.

1. The Marketing Maelstrom

In the past, marketing to children was a relatively low-budget affair, mostly concerned with toys and sweets. In the last decade or so, as electronic entertainment swelled, and especially as TVs and computers moved into children's bedrooms, it's become a multi-million-dollar business.

Children are now targeted not only through TV ads, but via internet pop-ups, emails, product placements in programmes and on websites, and in many other ways (see the box opposite).

The electronic media allow plenty of opportunities for the two great learning devices: imitation and repetition.

- If a product is cool (fun, fashionable, associated with characters or behaviour children find attractive), youngsters want to buy it in the hope that the 'cool' will rub off on them.
- Repeated bombardment through TV ads, pop-ups and so on means children quickly learn brand names, slogans and marketing messages.

Kids are growing older younger

One popular marketing strategy is KAGOY (Kids Are Growing Older Younger) – exploiting children's natural yearning to be more grown up.

To begin with, this latches on to pretend play: instead of using their imagination and a few dressing-up clothes, today's children are encouraged to want all sorts of paraphernalia, from fully equipped hairdressing salons to mini briefcases.

KAGOY has also affected the sort of dolls little girls covet. As well as Barbie with her endless accessories, there are now the very streetwise and extremely precocious Bratz dolls. The Bratz Secret Date Collection, marketed to six-year-olds, pairs each Bratz girl with a Bratz boy, and includes two champagne glasses and 'tons of date night accessories'.

All this attention to fashion opens the floodgates for much more spending. There is now a massive fashion industry for children of all ages, with styles that are increasingly adult, including 'sexy' underwear for little girls. Little wonder small children now have problems with body image (nearly three-quarters of seven-year-olds in a recent survey said they want to be slimmer because they believe it will make them more popular).

Selling to kids

- A company called Dubits recruits children on the web to be 'Dubit Informers'. The kids keep the company up to date on street trends and promote the latest 'cool' products in return for cash payments. The tag-line reads: 'Promote brands on the street for free stuff, prizes and cash.'
- In late 2006, children visiting Walmart's Toyland website were shown how to email their parents a list of the items they wanted for Christmas (an update of the traditional letter to Santa, but of course based on buying from Walmart).
- To create interest in a new snack product, an ad agency 'seeded' its promo figures (mutant fruit characters) at teeny-bopper concerts. They also featured the characters on websites visited by young teenagers, and on gifts of clothing to TV presenters. The idea was to make the characters popular with teenagers, so that younger children (the ad agency's target group) would see them as 'cool' and want to buy the product. It worked.

I always wonder whether the mothers who buy sexy clothing for their pre-teenage daughters and let them go out plastered in make-up are the same mothers who protest stridently about paedophiles . . . and whether they ever make the rather obvious connection.

Gotta catch 'em all

Another successful ploy is to turn children into rampant consumers by homing in on their natural urge to collect things. Pokémon's slogan 'Gotta catch 'em all' sums up the strategy, and there are now endless ranges of collectables to covet.

What's more, by emphasising natural differences in the interests of boys and girls, the marketeers exaggerate gender distinctions. Girls are directed towards girly-pink cutesy animals, fashion dolls and grooming products. Boys are lured to the mechanical, quirky, and competitive.

When you link collectability to fast-changing fashion you create endless opportunities for consumption. So now every film made for children spawns a vast array of consumer items, from console games to plastic figures in cereal packets or 'Happy Meals'. And no sooner has one collectable craze reached its peak than another begins.

The culture of cool

This marketing maelstrom affects children in another, very worrying way. The culture of cool it creates now rules the playground, so children's friendships and relationships are influenced by what they own. The wrong brand of food in your lunch box or a supermarket-label sweatshirt on your back can be social suicide.

Marketeers have also identified that it's natural for little boys to want to push the boundaries of acceptable behaviour. So they sell to boys using the concept of 'edgy cool'. This encourages an anti-authority stance that's at odds with the sort of behaviour parents and teachers try to encourage. But, as with KAGOY, the nature of marketing means constant upping of the ante – and the definition of 'edge' is becoming increasingly antisocial.

Playground culture has always existed, and it's always had a bit of an 'edge'. But in the past, it used to be children's own private world. It was influenced a little by children's books, comics and the media, but the children themselves maintained control. In many ways, it was an important part of growing up and learning how to leave the family nest. This organised invasion by marketing men is something completely new – and, from my point of view (as a parent and a teacher), very sinister.

> 'It's part of the official advertising worldview that your parents are creeps, teachers are weirdos and idiots, authority figures are laughable; nobody can really understand kids except the corporate sponsor.'
>
> Professor Mark Crispin Miller, psychologist

Kids as customers

There are three key reasons for business to invest heavily in marketing to children:

- ## Guilt money

Parents who fear they're not spending enough time with their kids often try to make up for their absence with expensive gifts or lots of pocket money. For marketeers it's a win-win situation. The parents have to work harder and longer to earn money to assuage their guilt. This means children spend more time with their electronic babysitters, so the marketeers can groom them to ask for more 'must-haves'.

- ## Pester power

Since children are now so well versed in 'what's hot and what's not', they're having ever greater influence on a range of family purchases:

cars, holidays, food, fashion, even cleaning products. Harassed parents often give in to pester power to keep the peace on shopping trips. In terms of larger items, they're often impressed by their child's knowledge about the product (and the 'guilt money' factor comes into play).

• Brand loyalty

If marketeers can win children for a brand when they're very young, they tend to stay loyal for life. So the aim is to get them recognising logos by two, asking for products by brand name by two and a half, and dedicated brand users by three and a half. Under the age of about eight, it's easy to convince a child that owning, eating or using a certain brand can make them happier and more successful.

Some parents' comments

'Lots of times you get home and it's "Can I have, can I have ..." whatever character it is. You open it up and they don't like it. They purely wanted it for the picture.'

'I have lost count of the number of tantrums I have had in Asda because I won't let the girls have a cereal just for the free gift.'

'I feel like I have to keep saying no because obviously with two children, not working, I just haven't got the money. And they want this and I'm forever going "No, no, no, no" and what the kids must think of me: "Oh I hate Mum because she never buys me anything." It does get really upsetting sometimes.'

'The advert shows you a little boy and his mum has given him this Dairylea slice, and he's saying how good his mum was, and this other poor boy has only got sandwiches. So his mum was really cruel, you know, and that's the wrong impression. That your mum's really cool because she buys you this crappy cheese, plastic cheese.'

'I need to ask if the advertising industry are comfortable spending millions of pounds to target children direct and then saying it's up to Mum and Dad to stand up to them.'

Quoted by kind permission of the Family and Parenting Institute (www.familyand parenting.org), from their publication *Hard Sell, Soft Targets*, 2004.

You are what you own?

Top psychologists employed by companies now work on ways to convince children their lives will be better if they own a certain product. The point, of course, is to sell products, not to ensure children's welfare.

'Kids are the most unsophisticated of all consumers; they have the least and therefore want the most. Consequently, they are in a perfect position to be taken.'

US marketing strategist James McNeal

'Advertising at its best is making people feel that without their product, you're a loser. Kids are very sensitive to that. If you tell them to buy something, they're resistant. If you tell them that they'll be a dork if they don't, you've got their attention. You open up emotional vulnerabilities and it's very easy to do with kids because they're the most emotionally vulnerable.'

Nancy Shalek, president of a major US advertising agency

'All of our advertising is targeted to kids. You want that nag factor so that seven year old Sarah is nagging mom in the grocery store to buy Funky Purple [ketchup]. We're not sure mom would reach for it on her own.'

Senior marketing manager, JH Heinz (quoted in *The Real Toy Story* by Eric Clarke)

'I love brands ... Brands not only tell me who I am, but also protect me from problems with the others in my class.'

11-year-old girl, quoted in a marketing manual

Money can't buy me love

Adults are usually well aware of the way marketeers constantly target us, and most of us just use the ads to help us make consumer choices. But young children aren't so sophisticated. If they absorb the message that 'you are what you own' at an early age, they're being set up for a lifetime of consumer-driven unhappiness. Psychological studies show that once people's basic material needs are met, real happiness comes not from owning more and more stuff but from

- strong and satisfying relationships with others
- opportunities to be creative
- the satisfaction of personal achievement
- a personal belief system that gives meaning to your life.

Fighting back

First of all, take control of the media in your home. Then talk to your child about marketing, consumerism and the difference between lifestyle and quality of life. Above all, talk about what *really* makes your child happy.

Ad talk

When you watch advertisements with children, talk about
- how the pictures, music, slogans and so on affect the way they feel and their attitude to the product being advertised
- whether the families in the ads are like real people
- what key advertising words like *fun, free, choice, love, natural, exciting* really mean – and can this product really provide them?
- what other tricks the marketeers are using to make you want to buy
- how well products they've tried have lived up to advertising promises.

As children grow more marketing-savvy, play 'What aren't they telling us?' What facts about the product have been missed out and why? For instance, when an ad says a food product is 'low in fat', might it contain other fattening ingredients, such as sugar?

In Sweden, they have banned marketing to children under the age of twelve. There's no reason why we can't do the same here – if enough parents believe we should.

Detoxing the consumer culture

Be warm:

- When young children first start watching commercial stations, play 'Spot the advertisements' to help them learn the difference between entertainment and marketing.
- Talk to your child about advertising, products and brands. Watch adverts together and discuss how the marketeers target people's hopes, fears and needs (see Ad talk, opposite).
- Video favourite programmes and teach how to fast-forward during ads.
- Do some consumer testing with your child and friends. Try 'blind tests' of food and drinks (e.g. baked beans, cereals, ketchup, soft drinks, colas) mixing famous brand products and supermarket own-labels. Can they tell the difference and how much does advertising influence their guesses?
- Involve children in making consumer decisions that use marketing information wisely, along with other considerations.
- Let them help make shopping lists and discuss food choices.
- Discuss other family purchases (cars, holidays, etc.), listening respectfully to their contributions.

Be firm:

- Monitor what children watch on TV, films and DVD – keep home entertainment in a shared area of the house and watch with them as often as possible.
- Keep an eye on ads and marketing, watch out for trends and be aware of the ways marketeers target children.
- Limit young children's viewing to non-commercial stations, such as CBeebies, or selected DVDs and videos.
- Demonstrate your distaste for predatory marketing to children – let your child know that marketeers are only interested in their money.
- Never give in to pester power. The earlier in a child's life you make a stand on this the better – but whatever the age, once you've decided, be firm. If you stick with it, your child will eventually realise it's not on.
- Don't fall into the 'guilt money' trap – presence is much more important than presents.
- Have clear, fair guidelines on money and spending. Decide what you will/won't pay for on a regular basis, then agree on levels of pocket money. If children want

and involving them in reasoned choices.

- Limit exposure to consumer culture by doing other things with your children: family outings, activities and hobbies, making things, and so on.

something extra to what you provide, teach them to save for it or wait for birthday/Christmas/ other regular present-giving time.

Further reading

Two books from the USA, giving more facts about the commercialisation of childhood: Juliet Schor, Born to Buy (Scribner, 2004) and Susan Linn, Consuming Kids: The Hostile Takeover of Childhood (NY New Press, 2005). An expose of the toy industry and its marketing methods: Eric Clarke, The Real Toy Story (Black Swan, 2007).

Useful websites

More information on a campaign against the commercialisation of childhood in the UK from: www.compassonline.org.uk/campaigns
US campaign about children and the media: http://www.childrennow.org/issues/media/index.html
Campaign against marketing of junk food to children: www.childrensfoodcampaign.org.uk

2. The Magic Box

Television has now been a fact of daily life for half a century. The big change over the last twenty years is the explosion of channels, providing a vast range of round-the-clock viewing. If TVs are in children's bedrooms, this viewing is unsupervised. We don't yet know the long-term effects of all this unlimited, unmonitored TV-watching, but experts in child development are becoming worried.

The electronic babysitter

The UK seems to lead the world in the number of very young children who now have TVs in their bedrooms. And this early introduction to wall-to-wall viewing seems to be affecting their language development (see page 90). What's more, primary headteachers complain that children now arrive at school with few experiences beyond staring at screens. It may be that children given access to unlimited TV in their earliest years are conditioned to use it for life as a default activity.

But the growth of electronic babysitting might also be connected with a range of learning disorders.

Screens and brains

ADHD (attention deficit hyperactivity disorder), dyslexia and autism are all called 'developmental disorders' because children who seem fine when they're born don't develop as expected. There's a physical explanation for all these conditions – glitches in children's brain structure or the chemical balance of the brain – and often they're hereditary. But most scientists believe aspects of lifestyle can add to the problem and in some children they might even create it. Research now suggests that excessive TV-watching could play a part, particularly in the first few years when neural pathways are forming in the brain.

- ## Attention deficit disorder

One research study looked at how watching TV affected children under the age of two. For every hour of TV they watched per day, there was a 9 per cent increase in attention deficit by the time the child was seven. The researchers thought that rapid changes of image on TV could make an immature brain go into overdrive – so when the child looks away from the screen, real life is boring.

- ## Dyslexia

Dyslexia is caused mainly by problems in processing the individual sounds of language (the c-a-t of *cat*). Children learn to process these sounds in the first year or so of life (see page 76), so they need plenty of real-life 'conversations' with adults to provide the language data. TV or video aren't adequate substitutes. And, of course, as children grow older, the availability of TV means they're less keen to practise reading.

- ## Autism (particularly Asperger's syndrome)

Children with a predisposition to autism find social contact difficult. They are thus often drawn to TV. A US study on under-threes recently found a strong link between autism and the number of hours spent watching TV. At the same time UK researchers were discovering that six- to eight-year-olds now prefer to look at a blank screen rather than a human face.

How a child has been socialised in the first few years of life will seriously affect whether he or she engages with people or engages with a television screen.

Professor Kevin Browne, forensic psychologist

In the USA, one in six children now has a developmental or behavioural disorder. No combined figures have been issued for the UK but, given that around one in ten children are diagnosed with dyslexia, ADHD and/or autism, the total must by now be similarly alarming.

Junk TV

For children of three and older, there are some excellent children's TV programmes that can both educate and entertain. And there are many other great programmes to share with adults. Sensible television-watching contributes hugely to child development and family life.

But sadly there's also a lot of dross. As TV channels have proliferated, all too often the extra airspace has been filled by junk – cheap programmes that appeal to the 'lowest common denominator' among the viewing public. And when one TV company finds a successful formula, others follow, each new version plumbing lower and lower depths.

Many parents now feel uneasy about many programmes shown during the day or early evening when children are watching, for instance:

- soap operas in which nasty behaviour or seedy lifestyles are increasingly seen as normal – sometimes even admirable
- reality TV and confessional chat shows, full of anger, bullying and confrontation
- cartoons and comedy programmes that ironically celebrate antisocial behaviour or cruelty (children under about eight don't understand irony – they think adults are *really* laughing at cruel or criminal acts)

- violent or sexually explicit programmes, and programmes with a lot of swearing.

Given that children learn by imitation, it's not surprising if nasty, bullying, confrontational behaviour is mirrored in playgrounds around the country, along with swear words and catchphrases such as 'Am I bovvered?'

> What are children to learn from *Big Brother*? They see a parade of lowest common denominator values, a celebration of our lowest farting, swearing, lusting and bullying instincts. It teaches them that nothing matters more than being famous.
>
> Geoff Barton, secondary headteacher

Challenging junk TV

You can, of course, ensure that your child doesn't watch such stuff. But if you do that, there's now a strong chance your child will be a social outcast at school. Out in the world, your child can't avoid mixing daily with others who've had access to junk TV.

So if you don't like it, the answer is to let the broadcasters know (see box, opposite). If enough parents voice their concern, they may take some action, but if you remain silent, the lowest common denominator may sink even lower.

Dealing with bad news

Another aspect of TV that can cause problems for children is the news. Graphic coverage of terrorist incidents, natural disasters, road accidents and hideous crimes can be destabilising for small children. At the same time, they fascinate children just as they do adults, so parents need to be aware of what they are seeing and hearing.

- For the under-sevens the best reaction is probably just to distract

You can contact broadcasters with praise about good programmes, and complaints about ones that concern you, at these addresses:

- BBC: www.bbc.co.uk 08700 100 222 or online www.bbc.co.uk/complaints
- ITV: www.itvplc.com 0870 600 6766 or dutyoffice@itv.com
- Channel 4: www.channel4.com 0207 306 8333
- S4C: www.s4c.co.uk 029 2074 1458 or hotline@s4c.co.uk
- Five: www.five.tv 0207 550 5555 or customerservices@five.tv
- BSkyB www.sky.com 0870 240 3000 or viewerr@bskyb.com

Make sure you give the following details:

- The title of the programme
- Date and time of transmission
- Name of TV or radio channel.

If you think a programme is damaging to children, you can also make complaints to Ofcom, the broadcasting regulator:

Ofcom's Contact Centre: 0845 456 3000 or contact@ofcom.org.uk

But as this watchdog appears to have very few teeth, it would also help to lobby your MP for more control of pre-watershed broadcasting.

them, give them a cuddle and reassure them warmly that you're there to take care of them.

- For older children, give sensible explanations why what they've seen on screen is unlikely to happen to them (e.g because we don't get earthquakes in the UK, because there are only a very very few bad people in the world).

But you can also use news items to help teach children about dangers and how to deal with them. One of the best ways to defuse anxiety is to revisit safety rules, work out family emergency procedures, and plan how you'd cope.

Heroes and villains

Children may also be influenced by the role models provided by TV and DVDs. The natural drive to imitate has always led children to seek out role models – from parents, siblings and teachers to heroes from history, sport or the media. But the role models most readily available on junk TV are 'celebrities' who are famous mainly for attention-seeking. The heroes of adult-rated DVDs tend to be violent or distinctly sleazy. None of this is the type of behaviour parents want to see their children copy.

Detoxing role models

- Make sure you, your partner and other 'adults in charge' are the sort of role models you want your child to copy.
- As children acquire heroes beyond the family, talk to them about the good qualities these heroes show. Discuss any aspects of the character your child may not understand (such as: why is it all right for Spiderman to fight people sometimes?).
- Keep an eye on the TV characters children admire. If they start imitating their speech or behaviour, talk about the character and why they like them. Don't be afraid to discourage your child if they've chosen an inappropriate hero.
- Similarly, when children show an interest in pop stars and other celebrities, talk about them and listen to your child's opinions. Encourage careful thought about people's worth. What characteristics does your child think are really important – and do these characters live up to their standards?
- If you're the single mother of a boy, do everything you can to provide a suitable male role model for your child (such as a family member, a male friend, a youth group leader) – someone who'll spend time with him and be there to give advice and support.

Celebrity role models are a constant presence, not just on junk TV, but on children's and music channels. Not surprisingly, when asked their ambitions for the future, most modern children now say they want to be rich and/or famous. And since celebrities achieve wealth and fame mainly through being egocentric and flamboyant, that's increasingly how children behave. The celebrity culture and the violent, sexually irresponsible 'hard men' (and women) on adult DVDs give little incentive to children to work hard at school or show concern for the needs of others.

Why not turn off the TV and . . .

If your child is watching too much TV, maybe it's turned into a default activity simply because there's nothing else to do? There are plenty of suggestions for filling family time throughout this book, but if you're looking for an immediate distraction you could suggest:

- going swimming or out for a bike ride
- easy cooking, like making biscuits
- going for a walk (dogs are useful here)
- going to the library and choosing a book to share
- asking some friends round – they could make a camp, stage a talent contest or some other sort of show, or go to the park.

If you've time and energy to spare, you could try:

- making a pile of family photographs and sorting them into albums/scrapbooks/biographies, or making a collage for your child's wall (while sorting, take the opportunity to reminisce and talk)
- getting out recipe books, and going through them together choosing meals you fancy cooking. Make menus for the week, take your child shopping for ingredients and do some shared cooking.
- exploring your local area. Get a map, and go on expeditions to find out about all the places you don't know (however unpromising they sound). Make sure you're properly equipped – camera,

notebook, food supplies – and collect information, pictures, souvenirs to make a scrapbook of your travels.

- throwing a Budget Party. With your child, decide on a theme (e.g. pirates, storyland, robots) and a budget (keep it low). Then enjoy planning and making costumes, decorations, food, invitations, activities – the lower your budget, the more ingenious you'll have to be. Invite a few of your child's friends and their parents, and enjoy yourselves.

Demonstrate to your child that, while it's fine occasionally to slump in front of a screen and be entertained, it's much more fun to entertain yourself and others. But if you don't switch off the magic box and make the effort to do something, you'll never discover the joy of living in the real world.

How to get the TV out of the bedroom

- The best way to keep technology out of bedrooms is never to let it in. Make a family rule that no one has a bedroom TV (at least until they are well into their teens).
- Choose an easy time for the transition, e.g. after a holiday when children watched little TV.
- Talk to your child about when and why you're removing the TV and why life will be better without it, e.g.
  - ⋆ there will be more time for talking, playing, having fun with parents and others
  - ⋆ the family will be able to share time together (including family viewing)
  - ⋆ it will help your child sleep better and do better at school.
- Listen to your child's views and respond as positively as possible, but don't get into an argument. The bottom line is: you've learned that bedroom TV can be harmful, you love your child and are protecting him or her from harm.

- Place the 'family TV' in a comfortable family space.
- Establish a pleasant bedtime routine (see page 35), involving a bedtime story. For older children, you could provide a CD or tape player for listening to audiobooks.
- Accept that you and other adults must be more selective about your viewing. Agree strategies for choosing what to watch, allow everyone a say and expect everyone to compromise. As always, adult role models count for a lot.
- When you remove the bedroom TV, ensure you and others are available to talk, play and have fun with your child (for instance, ask friends around to play).
- As time goes on, expect your child to play more independently.

Daily Mail, Tuesday, July 6, 2004

'It's long past his bedtime. Gently – he's got his lawyer with him.'

Detoxing TV

Be warm:

- Discuss your attitudes to TV with your partner and older children and devise policies that will work for you.
- Remember that TV is one of the great educative media, as well as being a wonderful source of entertainment; used appropriately, it will enrich your child's life.
- Your child is growing up in a world where TV and DVD-watching is the norm, so some viewing is important to ensure s/he is a 'child of the time'.
- Share TV with your child as much as possible. This means you act as a functioning family, rather than a disparate group of individuals, splintered off into different rooms of the same house.
- Talk about the TV/DVDs you watch together, e.g. marketing messages (see page 118), role models (see page 126) and the behaviour of people on screen.
- Find ways of rationing TV that suit your family, e.g. buy a TV guide every week, and let everyone circle the programmes they want to see (up to an agreed level), so you can just switch on when required and record any overlaps.

Be firm:

- Detoxing TV for children means looking at the viewing habits of the whole family. Adults have to model the sort of behaviour they expect from children.
- Keep the TV in a shared part of the house, and monitor children's media diet as carefully as you monitor the food they eat.
- Limit the amount of TV your child watches per day. If possible, don't let children under two watch at all; work out sensible limits (an hour or so per day?) for older children.
- Monitor all DVDs that come into your home. If you own DVDs that are unsuitable for children, keep them under lock and key.
- Don't let electronic entertainment become the default activity in your home – make it a rule that no family members automatically switch on the TV when they enter the room.
- Ensure TV watching is always purposeful, intentional and finite.
- Be prepared to make compromises about control of the airspace. Accept that this may mean a degree of sacrifice on your part.

- Perhaps you could have a special weekly 'family viewing evening' when everyone settles down together with popcorn and drinks for some viewing of DVDs or recorded programmes you all want to share.
- Make sure there are lots of real activities on offer to compete with electronic entertainment (see page 127) and make time to share these.

- Think of strangers on screen as you would think of them in real life. Never leave your children unsupervised in the company of anyone in whom you don't have utter confidence.
- Remember that the educational benefits of TV relate to material appropriate to the age range – a programme too old for your child to follow will be useless.
- Don't rely on V-chips or other devices to protect children from inappropriate programming – such technology is rapidly outdated. Use it to help, by all means, but take control yourself.

Further reading

Teresa Orange and Louise O'Flynn, *How to Stop your Kids Watching Too Much TV ...* (Hay House, 2007).

Aric Sigman, *Remotely Controlled: How Television is Damaging Our Lives and What We Can Do About It* (Vermilion, 2005).

Useful websites

www.mediamarchuk.org.uk
www.mediawatchuk.org

3. Virtual Worlds

Brave new world

Just like TV, electronic games and communication technology can be wonderful resources for your child:

- Games aren't just entertaining – they can help your child develop ways of thinking that s/he'll need in the technology-rich future.
- The web and internet give access to incredible amounts of information and expert knowledge.
- Using multimedia, your child can communicate ideas and understanding through images, video, animation, in ways we could only dream about a decade or so ago.
- Children can now make and keep friends locally and around the world through internet, MSN, blogs and texts.

Today's technology is likely to have an even greater impact on the course of human history than the invention of the printing press, and today's children are almost certainly standing on the threshold of a new Renaissance.

But as well as getting excited, parents must also be aware of the pitfalls of technology for their children. To thrive in the real world, children still need emotional resilience, social competence and the basic skills of reading and writing. We have to ensure that too much technology too soon doesn't threaten this real-life development.

> 'We know experience leaves its mark on the brain. We are bringing our children up in a very different environment from 20 years ago, where they press a button and get immediate feedback, where they spend hours in front of a screen. How can that not have a profound effect?'
>
> Baroness Susan Greenfield, neuroscientist and president of the Royal Institution

Real life versus virtual life

There's no doubt at all that children's brain development depends on warm human contact and first-hand experiences of the world around them (see Section I). Too early a start on virtual, computer-based activities is likely to damage that development. The younger the child, the more time s/he needs to spend:

- with real people, learning to communicate and get along
- exploring real life, starting at home, moving out into the local area and beyond.

Once basic neural pathways are laid down, there's a place for screen-based entertainment and communication. But if the foundations of children's learning are shaky, developmental problems loom. It's very possible that the same dangers listed for TV on page 122 apply to other screen-based entertainment.

Old and new literacy

Too much technology too young can make it more difficult to learn the 3Rs. In the early 1990s English primary schools introduced calculators, on the principle that modern children needed to know how to use them. Five years later they had to be withdrawn, because the children weren't learning how to add and subtract – they'd begun relying on calculators to do it for them.

Primary teachers have also noticed that children today have more trouble learning to read. As well as an alarming increase in special needs (see page 123), teachers report that children in general are more distractible and impulsive. This makes it harder for them to settle down and learn basic reading and writing skills. Children who arrive at school with poor language (also often connected with new technology – see page 77) find it even harder to learn.

Learning to read involves slowing down your mind. You have to process sounds into words and words into sentences, while at the same time making sense of what you're reading. Learning to write means slowing down even more, since you have to make the letters with your pencil, spell the words *and* sort out your grammar to express what you want to say.

On the other hand, electronics speed up the mind. Computer programmes encourage children to expect quick-fire quick-fix learning. If they're used to computer games, websites and push-button TV they're likely to find learning to read and write boring and laborious. Those who manage to get the basics often can't be bothered to practise – and true literacy takes years and years of practice.

Even the keenest of techies agree that you have to be able to read and write before you can take full advantage of electronic communications. Without basic literacy skills, access to worthwhile resources is very limited. My personal advice to parents is

- stick with real life for at least the first three years
- place firm limits (an hour a day *at the most*) on computer use until children are around eight or nine, and well on the way to being readers and writers
- limit time spent in virtual worlds until children are well into their teens.

Life's a game – play more

Computer game manufacturers have hijacked the language of play. Many children now think of play as something you do on a PlayStation and games as something you do on Gameboys. As well as distracting children (especially boys) from the real-life play they need (see page 56), too much virtual play may actually damage development.

In Japan (practically the spiritual home of new technology) there's real concern as literacy standards decline despite a fierce work ethic in schools. Between 2000 and 2004, the country dropped from eighth to fourteenth place in the international league table. Japanese newspapers report a steady rise in the number of children who don't read books at all.

Despite having 'interactive' all over the advertising, there's little genuine interactivity about virtual play, at least in the simple games and websites aimed at children. The child has only limited control, with no opportunity for true creativity. But children are easily fascinated, and so grow dependent on electronic gadgetry for entertainment, rather than learning to think independently.

Many young children also have access to violent games, such as Mortal Kombat and Grand Theft Auto III. In my research for Toxic Childhood I discovered that even though these games are 18-rated under-tens often persuade their parents that 'they're not all that bad' (apparently parents who are PlayStation virgins are easily fooled).

Parents need to know that modern computer violence of this kind is seriously nasty and extremely realistic – certainly not suitable for children. There is evidence that it encourages aggressive, violent behaviour and may well be having an adverse effect on boys' attitudes to women.

Once they're old enough to be self-regulating, teenagers can both learn and socialise through involvement in computer games. From a parental point of view, it's a question of making sure they grow up able to take advantage of the good stuff, rather than being distracted and damaged by too much bad stuff too early on.

Virtual friends and enemies

The same goes for virtual communication. Of course, you have to be able to read and write before you can email, text, blog or chat on MSN.

But if children get bogged down in text-speak as soon as they can master a keyboard, there's a good chance their literacy skills will stay at that level. True literacy takes practice, and too much time spent on virtual friendships can seriously distract from that practice.

Parents are often wary about virtual friendships because of stories of paedophiles grooming children on the internet. It's well established that some people in chatrooms are not who they claim to be (a journalist posing as 12-year-old 'Tina Bell' logging in to a chatroom a few years ago was immediately contacted by dozens of predatory men), and both children and parents need to be alert to this. But there are many other problems involved in virtual communication:

- Blogs, chatrooms and mobiles are used by marketeers promoting products by pretending to be kids making genuine recommendations.
- Children may stumble across websites or chat among people promoting anything and everything, from extreme political views to suicide clubs.
- Correspondents nearer home can be dangerous, too. If children fall out with friends, chatroom or text-based bullying can cause great distress.

Children who find it difficult to make friends are particularly vulnerable to cyber-bullying . . . and, ironically, the more time they spend making virtual friendships, the less good they're likely to be at real-life friendship.

Web-based chat isn't the same as face-to-face real-life conversation; on the net, you can be whoever you choose, and control when and how often you communicate, melting into cyberspace if anything goes wrong. Texting is also disembodied, and thus safer than real conversation. So it's not surprising that many children prefer virtual friendship to the cut and thrust of real life. But if they withdraw into a virtual world, they'll never learn the social skills that underpin successful adulthood.

We just don't talk any more

It's not just the children who are retreating into virtual worlds. Parents are often lured away from the family too:

- Laptops, BlackBerries and mobiles mean work has a habit of spreading into home life.
- TV is easy to switch on, provides rapid relaxation, and tends to draw you in whether you're really interested or not.
- Email and web-browsing expand to fill the given space – you sit down and, hey presto, an hour has just flown by.
- Ipods allow you to frequent your own little world, oblivious of what's going on around you.

We have to be warm and firm with ourselves about this, and recognise that real life is more important than virtual unreality.

Detoxing electronic communication

Be warm:

- The web is a fantastic resource for parents and children. Check out the websites on page 140 to find ways of using it positively.
- Computer games can be great fun and some are mind-expanding. Help your child choose wisely and play new games with him/her so you know what they are.
- Email, MSN-messaging, texting and

Be firm:

- Keep computers, console games and so on in family space, and make sure you know exactly what your child is doing on them.
- Make sure you know as much as possible about any hardware and software that comes into your home. If you aren't able to put in the time and energy to find out about an electronic

so on are a part of the digital world your child was born into – encourage sensible, limited electronic communication, but also make sure your child is good at face-to-face communication.

- Ensure your child knows that your key concern is his/her welfare. Explain the advantages and dangers of growing up in a virtual world.
- Demonstrate to your child how to behave on the net and how to avoid dangers, just as in the real world. Again, check out detailed suggestions on websites, and recheck them every so often to keep up to date.
- Let your child teach you. Sometimes, s/he will know about new technology from school or friends and can pass on knowledge to you – a great way for you to learn and your child to feel important.
- Ensure your child knows that if s/he encounters anything in the electronic village that makes him or her feel uncomfortable, embarrassed or worried, s/he should let you know.

product, don't let it over the threshold.

- Agree time limits for logging on, playing, messaging, etc each day, and stick to them. (Negotiate extra time for homework on an ad hoc basis.)
- Make sure your child knows *never* to open a suspicious email, click a suspicious hyperlink, respond to unexpected messages on mobile phones or fill in any forms on the internet without checking with you. (Give dire warnings about viruses that knock out the system, how you could be spammed to death, etc.).
- Tell your child *never* to give out your real address or phone number to anyone they meet in the electronic village.
- Use software and 'web-nannies' to limit email access and so on if you wish, but remember that such technology is rapidly outdated. So don't trust technology to protect your family – maintain control yourself.

Pigeon post

I know from experience how easy it is for electronic communication to become a default activity. For about a year, whenever I found myself with nothing to do, I'd think 'Oh – I'll just go and check the email.' Once logged on, I could waste ages on trivial correspondence, quite forgetting my family. My addiction was cured by a friend comparing me to a pigeon.

She reminded me about the psychologist B.F. Skinner, who experimented on the effect of rewards on learning. He gave his pigeons a grain of food every time they pecked at a particular spot. Skinner found that if he rewarded a pigeon every time it pecked it took the food for granted, and pecked only when it was hungry. If he hardly ever gave a reward, the pigeon lost interest. But if he gave intermittent, unpredictable rewards, pigeons would peck enthusiastically – some pecked their beaks blunt.

Emails are intermittent rewards; you never know when there might be a nice one. The same applies to mobile calls, texts, chat messages. The family, on the other hand, is always around, so they can be taken for granted. But the difference between pigeons and parents is that pigeons are stupid, while parents can recognise how they're being manipulated by circumstances, and act to put it right.

Here's a quote from another mother who's thrown off the chains of pigeonhood: 'I'm a typical 21st-century mum, juggling my priorities regarding my children, family time and my work interests ... Having had my first child at 33 I found it terribly difficult to slow down to a pace of life that didn't bring the professional recognition I had grown used to.

'Since reading [*Toxic Childhood*], I am confident that I am actually normal! I'd been sending emails, browsing the web and taking phone calls during my time with the children, most of which could always wait until later, but somehow made me feel as though I had a sense of control over something at least. But now I have consciously switched off the PC until the children go to bed and deliberately let phone calls go unanswered, so that it doesn't interrupt my time with the children. Actually, not having children bickering while I am on the phone or distracting me is such a release, as there are very few things which they now need to fight for my attention.'

Useful websites

www.cyberangels.org (international parents organisation – very helpful).

www.chatdanger.com (magazine approach to issues, including phones, chatrooms, instant messaging).

www.kidsmart.org.uk (basic safety advice, user-friendly presentation).

www.getnetwise.org (gives list of tools for blocking websites, etc.).

www.childnet-int.org (international campaign helping to make the internet safe) .

www.thegoodwebguide.co.uk (a good first port of call for reviews of websites on any subject).

Conclusion

There are billions of parents in the world. Of the many hundreds I've met over the last few years, almost all agreed with the main points made in *Toxic Childhood*, so presumably there are plenty more out there who feel the same. If they all got together, parent power could detoxify childhood – for all children – in no time.

But then ... parents today are too busy, too bombarded, too beset to organise some sort of worldwide social revolution. And anyway, isn't it more important to put one's own house in order first?

The point is that even putting one's own house in order involves getting together. Throughout this book, we've seen that detoxing your own children's lives involves collaboration with other parents. How are 21st-century mothers (and others looking after small children at home) going to stay sane unless they find other adults to talk to? How can we eat shared meals unless we find someone to share them with? How are parents to arrange for their children to play outside unless they collaborate with other parents?

The lesson I've learned from the last

four years is that detoxing childhood means investing our energy in parental collaboration rather than parental competition. If we want to ensure our children grow up healthy and happy, bright and balanced, we have to work together.

Parent power

In suggesting an upsurge of 'parent power', I don't mean some sort of national organised movement. I just mean parents taking back control of the business of raising their children, and finding their own ways to overcome the damaging side effects of 21st-century life. All parents have one overriding interest in common – the wellbeing of our children. And in order to ensure that wellbeing, we have to step outside the competitive consumer culture, start talking about the problems confronting modern families, and find collaborative ways to sort them out.

It's no good waiting for someone else to sort out toxic childhood syndrome for us. Big business just wants to sell us more stuff. Governments – no matter how much they might want to help – simply strangle us in red tape. Experts can offer advice through books, websites, TV programmes and all the wonders of modern technology, but they don't know anything about your child, your family, your neighbourhood. There's no one-size-fits-all solution to bringing up children.

In the end, as usual, it's up to parents to sort out the mess. But what I've found fascinating, as I travel about meeting parents who are already tackling the problem, is how much fun they seem to be having. It's enjoyable for me, too, listening to their ideas and stories. Three years researching *Toxic Childhood* and unravelling all the many dangers facing children left me a tad depressed. But a year on the road – talking to parents, teachers and, of course, children – has returned me to the sunny side of the street. Part of the solution to our problems is definitely to get out more.

The birthday party competition

When I speak at parents' meetings I sometimes suggest people talk about birthday parties. Once upon a time, these were simple affairs: games, jelly, ice cream, a birthday cake with candles and a good time had by all. But competitive consumerism changed all that.

All too often now, parties are occasions for vast and largely pointless expenditure. In some circles, every child in the class has to be invited (leading not only to an obscenely large pile of presents for the birthday child, most of which are abandoned within minutes, but also a ridiculous social calendar). In lots of places, parents feel there's a constant upping of the ante in terms of themes, excursions and entertainers. Almost everywhere there's the utter misery of wondering what to put in the party bags.

There may be the odd parent who enjoys the birthday party competition, but most people I meet say they absolutely hate it. And as one who's turned up to countless children's parties for over 30 years, I'm pretty sure the children aren't getting all that much out of it, either. In many cases, conspicuous consumption seems to have taken over from fun.

The answer, fairly obviously, is to try to maximise the fun of parties while cutting out the competitive element. And that involves collaboration. At one meeting – over a glass of wine in the interval – I overheard three mums discussing throwing a joint party. At another they were agreeing to dump the party bags. On one occasion I even heard someone squeal: 'Oh yes … let's have jelly!'

If you fancy tackling the party problem in your neck of the woods, have a look at www.birthdayswithoutpressure.com

Starting the ball rolling…

So how do you get parents together so they can start talking? Recently I was asked to speak about *Toxic Childhood* in Sevenoaks in Kent, and I asked the parents who'd organised it what had inspired the event.

Apparently, one mother who'd recently arrived back after living in France was struck by the low profile and lack of support for motherhood in the UK. In Paris, there were monthly meetings in a café, organised by a council-run families association, where over a cup of coffee a specialist gave a free talk about some aspect of child development. There'd be an opportunity to ask questions, chat and discuss points with other mothers.

When invited out for a coffee by a mum from her daughter's school, she confided her concerns and met with complete agreement. So together they invited more mothers for a glass of wine, broached the subject . . . and within half an hour had decided to set up their own parents' group, to meet once a month in a local café. 'Frankly, we were amazed and delighted at the reaction. Everyone we spoke to was immediately enthusiastic about the idea, including several of the local headteachers.'

Thanks to new technology, they were able to invite me along to kick the whole thing off with an inaugural lecture on *Toxic Childhood*, and to email fliers to all the local schools, parenting magazines and so on. Most schools were immediately supportive and photocopied the fliers to go home in book bags and up on noticeboards. They

approached local coffee shops, playgroups, GP surgeries and libraries to put up posters. Nearly 200 people turned up to the lecture. They all took home fliers about forthcoming meetings, asking for ideas for future talks, and offering to keep in email contact.

So two people started the snowball of trust and collaboration rolling, a handful of activists gave it a push, and now they have a flourishing group called 'Promoting Parenting' with a database of 70 members and a waiting list of local specialists (headteachers, psychologists, nursery and parenting experts) who would like to come and talk. Email means they can invite local and national speakers and keep in touch with members quickly and cheaply. While the talks provide a focus to each meeting, the main point is for parents to meet up, chat and swap ideas.

There are similar stories of collaboration scattered about this book. Everywhere I go, as well as finding people who think 'nothing can be done', I find others who've got together to do something:

- Some mums in Yorkshire (who met in the maternity ward) formed a club to help each other return to pre-pregnancy weight, but found it has grown into a long-term child-raising support system.
- In Wiltshire, a group of fathers organised a monthly breakfast club in a local pub, to hear invited speakers and swap ideas – it's usually a sell-out, with dads from a wide mixture of backgrounds.
- In Watford, a mother told me about a group of friends who met through the National Childbirth Trust, formed a mutual support group, and still meet up regularly even though their children have all grown up and left home.

Making contact

But what if you haven't stumbled across someone with whom you fancy wielding a bit of parent power? Well, there are almost certainly other people who share your interests at antenatal classes, toddler groups or in the school yard. The only way to find out is to ask them.

Don't be put off by other parents' apparent competence and organisation. Everyone puts on a front, and every parent I've ever met turned out to be struggling just as hard as me, no matter how swanlike and serene they appeared on the surface. But people do like to be asked for advice, so that can be a good way to introduce yourself. Or perhaps you could ask whoever's in charge (group leader, teacher, headteacher) if they could organise a meeting that would bring parents together – perhaps arrange a talk with time for discussion? The many teachers who attend *Toxic Childhood* presentations would be delighted to get something started in their schools.

It helps people make connections if there's a specific topic to talk about, otherwise you can just end up aimlessly chatting about last night's TV. Not that there's anything wrong with aimless chat – it's an important part of the social glue that makes collaboration possible – but sometimes one just has to cut to the chase.

And there are plenty of chases for 21st-century parents to cut to. Among those arising in this book are:

- How can we provide healthy family (or, at least, shared) meals, eaten at a regular time every day?
- How can we sort out work-life balance so that parents and children can have family time together?
- How do we protect children from predatory marketeers, junk TV and strangers online?
- How can we provide the best sort of childcare at each stage of children's development?

All well worth pursuing. All you need is to find other people interested in solving the problem that's bothering you at the moment.

Out to play

One of the most pressing issues in many local areas is how to detoxify outdoor play (see pages 51-58). Unless we find some way to ensure children can play outdoors safely with other children of the same age, and with only light-touch supervision, their overall development is likely to be seriously impaired.

The first hurdle is for adults to get over their fret about 'stranger danger' (see page 53), and discussing your fears with other people can be very helpful in this respect. On the other hand, anxiety thrives in silence. Next there's the question of ensuring that children are safety-conscious. Talking to other parents can help you sort out the best rules and boundaries for your neck of the woods. But then comes the greatest hurdle: ensuring that the great outdoors is as safe as possible. This isn't usually too great a problem in rural areas, but in cities and suburbs there's traffic to contend with. Even here, though, parents have told me stories of finding a way through.

Safer streets

A mother in north London told me how the people on her estate got together about ten years ago when the build-up of traffic meant parents were becoming scared to let their children out to play: 'It was one mum who got it going, really – she complained to the council and they wouldn't do anything to calm the traffic, so she organised a demonstration. We did that thing of keeping crossing the road – you know, pedestrians lining up to cross, so the traffic comes to a standstill. It backed up for miles!'

They won their traffic-calming measures so the road was safe again, but found that another other advantage of the campaign had been that it forged a real sense of community. 'And we've tried to keep it up – we're not in and out of each other's houses all the time or anything, but we try to keep an eye out for all the kids, not just our own, and to welcome new people that move in. It's a bit of a run-down-looking estate, actually, but it's a great place to live. I wouldn't want to move anywhere else.'

I heard a similar story from inner London, where a father invited other parents from his street round for a drink. 'We talked about how children don't play out any more, and agreed to keep an eye on all our kids so they could go out.' They worked out boundaries and rules, including very strict rules about road safety. 'My two girls are playing outside now with some other children – we can keep an eye through the window. And they all know they can go to any of the houses if they're worried.'

'Ah yes,' people say when I tell these stories. 'But we couldn't do anything about the streets round here. They're past saving.' In which case, of course, parents need to look further afield to ensure safe outdoor places for their children to play – parks, playing fields, local wild places ... A group of parents at a preschool in the north-east raised money to rent an unused allotment and turned it into a 'wilderness play area', where children can make dens and mud pies, climb trees and fences and – with adult supervision – have occasional bonfires (great for getting rid of household rubbish). They even grow a few vegetables.

Higher authorities

What all the success stories I hear have in common is that the starting point is parental collaboration. When people leave it to 'higher authorities' to sort out their children's play spaces, they're lucky if they get a square of tarmac with some bland plastic play equipment or a patch of grass for kicking a football around. And in many cases, these days, they're unlucky. All over the country, playing fields have been sold off because local councillors, many of whom are not parents, didn't see them as important.

Yet local councils exist to serve local people, and most of the voters in any locality are parents or grandparents. So if the area around you has nowhere fit for children to play, you'll need your local councillor to help sort it out. It's best if you go armed with a wish list, so brainstorm first – and then make democracy work with you and for you. If it doesn't, you could try

- taking direct action (like the parents who crossed the road, and rebuilt their community by doing so)
- going to the local newspaper – they'd *love* to receive a letter about how Councillor Bloggs is stopping little children from going out to play. (You might even get the front page!)

To put out the word about any project you're trying to get off the ground, you could contact the local newspaper or freesheet; they're always on the look-out for local stories. If you give a mobile number or email address, like-minded souls can get in touch.

Or, like the mums in Sevenoaks, you could do a poster campaign. This has the added advantage that you meet lots of people when you go round asking to put up the posters. Since many of them are likely to be parents or grandparents themselves, you can gather a fair number of recruits to the cause before you've even started. (Another advantage of new technology is that almost anyone can design really good posters.) You never know, you could end up going national ...

Detoxing junk TV

Mothers Pippa Smith and Miranda Suit are deeply worried about the effects of junk TV on children. As long-time members of a national pressure group, by 1999 they were frustrated that the situation just seemed to get worse and worse. So they took to the streets, starting with a demo outside Channel 4.

Despite having seven school-age children to look after between them, they set up a group called Mediamarch and, for the last seven years, have organised annual marches on Trafalgar Square. In 2005 they handed a petition of 121,000 signatures to Downing Street, calling for stronger regulation of the media. So far politicians haven't listened – but if enough people turn up on their marches, maybe they will. Try www.mediamarch.org.uk to find out the date of the next one.

Give us back our game

Paul Cooper is a father who coaches under-10s football and worries about the over-competitiveness now widespread on both the pitch and the touchline (where the behaviour of some parents is appalling). Paul reckons it's more important for children to learn to love football, rather than being drilled with skills, and that the greatest players honed their talents with 'street football', played for the sheer joy of it. (As Bobby Charlton said in 1966, 'The World Cup wasn't won on the playing fields of England. It was won in the streets.')

To revive the fun of street football, Paul had the idea of a Fun Football Day in June 2007 promoting '4v4' games (small-scale matches combining light-hearted competition with enjoyment). When he set up a website – www.giveusbackourgame.org.uk – he was bombarded with messages of support from professional footballers and with offers of money to promote the cause. Detoxing Childhood went to press before the day, but this is clearly a network just waiting to grow ...

Family politics

There are plenty of issues parents can sort out between themselves. But on other occasions politics raises its ugly head. For instance, if you believe we need:

- laws making companies pay more than lip service to work-life balance
- changes to the way we care for preschoolers
- improvements in primary education
- regulation to rein in aggressive marketing
- action to control the content of pre-watershed broadcasting
- some way of limiting the information children can access on the internet

then you'll need political help to get it.

Most people loathe the very idea of politics, and would run miles to avoid entanglement. And in the last 20 years or so, politicians have become so far removed from real life that it's difficult to imagine how they can engage productively with genuine human problems. But when our children's welfare is involved, parents have no option. *We have to make politicians help detoxify childhood.*

There are various ways to engage their attention on an issue:

- put your name to a petition – if enough people sign up to something, even the most self-serving politician can't ignore it
- write to your MP – if s/he gets enough letters, s/he'll have to start asking questions in Westminster
- join a campaign – log on to a website, turn up to meetings, go on marches, help think up clever ways of drawing attention to your cause.

The next time elections come round (local or national), make it clear that you'll be voting not just on your own behalf, but on that of your child (and other children). Go to election meetings, write, email, and put your case when canvassers turn up on your doorstep.

In the end, it's a numbers game. Which is why parent power has a real chance of changing the world for the better. There are millions of parents in this country: millions of votes. Parental love transcends party politics. If parents connect, networks form, and information spreads around the networks, parents could win in any numbers game.

It has to be worth a try. And if every parent gives it a try, to help solve his or her family's particular problems, there's a really strong chance it would work.

Building a network

Parent power is all about connecting. We're like all those individual cells in a human brain: there are billions of us, but we don't actually achieve anything until we make connections with other cells. But once the connections get started, they can create a completely new network.

This, of course, is where modern technology really comes into its own. The web is the ultimate in connectivity, giving everyone access to (a) everyone else's good ideas about everything and (b) a place to meet other local people with similar interests. With half an hour's Googling, you can mine enormous amounts of information about what's possible; the web addresses given throughout this book are a good starting point for specific issues. And there are now plenty of networking websites to consult.

- **Citizens Online** (www.citizensonline.org.uk) shows how to use the web to enrich real-life communities. Examples range from children running special ICT classes for their grandparents to parents using the net to fight school closures.
- **The BBC Action Network** (www.bbc.co.uk/dna/actionnetwork/) is an easy way to find organisations and individuals who share your interests. If you want advice on some sort of community action, they'll probably be able to put you in touch with someone who knows the ropes.
- **Big Wide Talk** is a charity helping parents solve problems – lots of ideas, advice, starting points: www.bigwidetalk.org.uk.
- **The Alliance for Childhood** website acts as an umbrella for groups concerned with detoxing childhood. As this book went to press, it already featured a number of campaigns arising from the toxic childhood debate, and is available to host more: www.allianceforchildhood.org.uk.

Mind the gap

There's one other important aspect of 21st-century life to take into account, one that could have a profound effect on your children's future. Any parents who pick up this book are probably already taking steps to detox their own children's lives. But those children have to grow up and live in the same society as the growing ranks of children whose parents can't or won't take authoritative control of their lives.

For most of the 20th century, the gap between rich and poor in the UK was growing smaller. The grinding poverty of the past had all but disappeared, and children from poor families had a good chance, through education and hard work, of moving into the middle classes. But somewhere around the early 1980s, things began to change. The gap began to widen again.

Today's gap between haves and have-nots can't be measured simply in material terms. Many of today's 'poor' have plenty of consumer goods like widescreen TVs and cars. Instead, it's a gap in education, life chances and hope. Children at the bottom of this heap now have little chance of moving up and out, and their parents are unaware of – or perhaps too locked in their own hopeless lives to care about – the ill effects of toxic childhood.

So children in poor, poorly educated families tend to have unhealthy diets, chaotic lifestyles, plenty of exposure to junk TV, marketing messages and computer violence, and little parental discipline as they get older. Their toxic childhood erupts into toxic adolescence. Britain now has the highest levels of teenage pregnancy in Europe, the highest teenage rate of sexually transmitted diseases, the largest youth prison population and the biggest teenage problem with alcohol and drug abuse. Meanwhile, poor and poorly educated families tend to have lots of children, while the wealthy and well-educated have fewer every year. It doesn't take a mathematical genius to work out where this is taking us. Unless we act soon, our children will have to survive in an increasingly toxic world.

'In our inner cities and poorer areas, we are rearing a generation without basic moral values. It's not the children's fault. They are, after all, children. It's ours: we who are their parents, their teachers and their guardians have simply let them down.'

Shaun Bailey, founder of MyGeneration, working with emotionally deprived children in north London

> 'When you put that kind of kid near your child, who may be well cared for, your child is going to have to up the ante to survive in the school playground. These kids heighten the temperature of violence, so other kids have to become violent. Violence then becomes the normal currency, and this culture spreads like a virus.'
>
> Camilla Batmanghelidjh, Founder of Kids Company for emotionally deprived children in south London

So just detoxing our own children's lives isn't enough. Whether through social conscience or enlightened self-interest, we have to notice the widening gap and take steps to close it.

The breakdown of trust

Within the last 20 or so years, there's been a serious breakdown of trust in society. It's easy to come up with reasons for this. For instance:

- In a global village, where work opportunities are widespread and travel is easy, we no longer stay in the area where we grew up. This means people don't know much about their neighbours, and since everyone is rushing around at 'electric speed' these days, there isn't time to get to know them. Lack of knowledge breeds lack of understanding, which breeds suspicion.
- Many neighbourhoods now house a mixture of people from very different cultures, often speaking different languages. Differences in the way people look, act and speak deepen the suspicion.
- Age-old values about behaviour (often handed down through religious traditions) have faded away and been replaced by laws, which are open to abuse. People are now often so frightened of litigation that we keep our heads down, rather than confronting antisocial behaviour or offering support in dodgy situations.

- A 'culture of blame', fed by lawyers and the media, means families often seek to protect their own interests at the expense of others (and often by blaming them).
- Media coverage of violent crime, unfair litigation and 'stranger danger' makes everyone more fearful, and constantly stirs up the unwholesome mix.

Explanations are cheap. It's much less easy to come up with solutions, and all political parties are now frenziedly looking for ways to rebuild communities.

Rebuilding communities

But communities can't be rebuilt from the top down – they have to grow, from the grassroots upwards. And the grassroots of any community are its families. This is, in fact, how communities came about in the first place – families banding together to protect and provide for their children. It's at the root of our tribal nature. Indeed, it goes much further back – to the pack instinct of higher animals. In moving forward as members of the virtual global village, we can't ignore our deep human need for real-life social engagement and support.

Parents may well be the only group who can rescue society from its current malaise. We have a real and serious stake in the future. Being a parent isn't just about looking inward, at the children in the centre of your own family. It's about looking outward, at the world where those children – and future generations of children – will grow and live.

For the sake of our children (and their children), we need to forge not only 21st-century families, but 21st-century communities – *authoritative* communities that can support authoritative parenting, for all children, not just the lucky ones.

Why can't we leave it to the state?

Politicians are not exactly famed for their understanding of child development. Left to their own devices they tend to focus on data, statistics and economics, which they *can* understand. In recent years, this has led to the bureaucratisation of the childcare industry and education system described in Section II. While we undoubtedly need new childcare solutions for the 21st century, the effects of this nanny-stateism could well be helping to break down communities, rather than building them up.

But politicians exist to serve the people who elect them. If we want them to help us forge successful families and authoritative communities, parent power could make them get on with it.

- Government could provide information about child development through secondary-school citizenship classes, antenatal and postnatal services, preschools and primary schools.
- It could help parents to meet and work together by providing free accommodation (schools or other council-owned properties) and access – *if requested* – to experts, such as playworkers, planners, childcare and education specialists.
- It could support parent groups in furthering their aims through local and national democracy.

Some very disadvantaged parents may need more intrusive support, but most parents just need to be informed and empowered to get on with the job themselves.

On a national and international level, government could turn its attention to the regulation of the electronic media, finding some way to ensure that the malign influences on children are reined in.

The adult alliance

Until very recently, an unwritten 'adult alliance' supported all parents in raising their children. Youngsters outside the home were expected to behave with respect towards their elders, and in return adults would keep an eye on children's welfare. Even complete strangers sometimes stepped in to warn about unsafe or unkind behaviour, or to protect children from obvious harm. And parents would, on the whole, support other adults. If a neighbour, teacher or other respectable adult accused a child of misbehaving, most parents would take their part and the children would be given short shrift.

As trust and respect broke down in society, this adult alliance faded and in many areas now it's all but disappeared. Rifts have developed between the groups who have, in the past, protected all children's interests – parents, teachers, traders, the old folk in the neighbourhood who have time to keep a watch on the streets. The way to start building authoritative communities is to revive the adult alliance.

Which brings me back to the beginning of the chapter. All parents need support in bringing up their children, so we need to talk to each other and to anyone else who can help. By making social connections, we start building networks that can improve life for all children. The alliances we forge between adults, for children's good, will help create the authoritative communities society needs. In a fragmenting world, it takes a leap of faith to extend trust and respect to people you don't know. But by making the effort, parents start rolling the snowball that can build a new adult alliance for the 21st century. By doing the best for our children, we can change the world.

Reviving the adult alliance

Be warm (with your child, yourself and everyone else):

- Be a good role model. Always
    * show by your behaviour that you think about other people's feelings and needs
    * treat *everyone* with respect
    * abide by social conventions, e.g. polite language.
- Try smiling and saying 'Good morning!' to people you meet. It's very gratifying when they respond.
- Assume other people are goodhearted and trustworthy unless you have definite evidence to the contrary. Teach your child to trust other people . . . BUT explain that some people aren't as nice as they seem. Teach your child never to suffer behaviour that makes him or her uncomfortable or frightened, but to tell you about anything worrying.
- Explain that older people are less fit than younger ones, and age earns concessions (such as a seat on the bus or extra tolerance of irritating behaviour).
- When your child is small, help him or her avoid disturbing others when distressed by removing yourselves – this also allows you to calm your child more easily.

Be firm (with your child, yourself and everyone else):

- Be a good role model. Always
    * be polite and respectful when putting your point of view.
    * acknowledge your responsibilities to other people.
    * politely expect others to respect your point of view and acknowledge your rights.
- While assuming people are trustworthy, maintain sensible scepticism, and always model intelligent safety precautions. Teach your child to do the same.
- Don't let other people's bad behaviour put you off behaving well.
- If your child is disrespectful to an adult, apologise and show your disappointment to your child. Explain later to what was wrong with the behaviour and why.
- When your child is small, if you're in a public place (e.g. restaurant, church service, shop, museum, any sort of performance) position yourself so you can make a quick getaway if your child cries or misbehaves.
- If other people question your child's behaviour, listen respectfully to their point of view. Bear in mind that your child is not

- Make social contacts with other adults in your community and, when an opportunity arises, talk about how important the adult alliance is. Listen to their opinions and concerns and try to draw them into reviving the alliance.
- If your child complains that an adult is behaving unpleasantly, talk it over and think about why they might be acting that way.
- Teach your child the art of keeping a low profile to avoid incurring the displeasure of particularly grumpy adults. Try to maintain a cordial relationship with grumpy adults so you can sort out any problems pleasantly if possible.

perfect – even the loveliest children lie to protect themselves from parental wrath. Try to imagine how you'd feel if someone else's child had behaved in that way to you.
- If an adult seems to have it in for your child, teach your child how to keep out of that person's way.
- If the problem persists, keep a log of incidents. Then if things escalate, you have some evidence.
- Ask to discuss the problem with the adult and listen respectfully (see above) with a view to finding a solution. Bring in outside agencies only as a last resort.

For four and a half years, I've been up to my ears in scientific research papers, academic articles and data about the effects of modern life on child development. But when I was explaining it all to a young father in Glasgow, he narrowed his eyes and said, 'So what you mean is that neuroscience has caught up with what Granny used to say?'

Yes, indeed. In terms of what children need, all that hard-won women's wisdom passed down through the ages still applies today. For children to grow up bright and balanced they need, first and foremost, love. They also need real food, real play, first-hand experiences and time and attention from the loving adults in their lives. As they grow, they'll also learn from others beyond the family, so we need to know that an adult alliance will support their emotional and social wellbeing, not only in our local area but throughout the global electronic village.

It shouldn't be too difficult for a modern technological society to achieve this. Human beings have solved much tougher problems in the past – it just takes collective will. This book is one mother's attempt at a snowball. Perhaps you could roll it a little further ...?

Or, of course, you could roll your own ...